# THINGS OF
# REDEEMING
# WORTH

*Scriptural Messages
and World Judgments*

# RELIGIOUS STUDIES CENTER PUBLICATIONS

## BOOK OF MORMON SYMPOSIUM SERIES

The Book of Mormon: The Keystone Scripture

The Book of Mormon: First Nephi, The Doctrinal Foundation

The Book of Mormon: Second Nephi, The Doctrinal Structure

The Book of Mormon: Jacob through Words of Mormon, To Learn with Joy

The Book of Mormon: Mosiah, Salvation Only through Christ

The Book of Mormon: Alma, The Testimony of the Word

The Book of Mormon: Helaman through 3 Nephi 8, According to Thy Word

The Book of Mormon: 3 Nephi 9–30, This Is My Gospel

The Book of Mormon: Fourth Nephi through Moroni, From Zion to Destruction

## MONOGRAPH SERIES

Nibley on the Timely and the Timeless

Deity and Death

The Glory of God Is Intelligence

Reflections on Mormonism

Literature of Belief

The Words of Joseph Smith

Book of Mormon Authorship

Mormons and Muslims

The Temple in Antiquity

Isaiah and the Prophets

Scriptures for the Modern World

The Joseph Smith Translation: The Restoration of Plain and Precious Things

Apocryphal Writings and the Latter-day Saints

The Pearl of Great Price: Revelations from God

The Lectures on Faith in Historical Perspective

Mormon Redress Petitions: Documents of the 1833–1838 Missouri Conflict

Joseph Smith: The Prophet, the Man

## SPECIALIZED MONOGRAPH SERIES

Supporting Saints: Life Stories of Nineteenth-Century Mormons

The Call of Zion: The Story of the First Welsh Mormon Emigration

The Religion and Family Connection: Social Science Perspectives

Welsh Mormon Writings from 1844 to 1862: A Historical Bibliography

Peter and the Popes

John Lyon: The Life of a Pioneer Poet

Latter-day Prophets and the United States Constitution

View of the Hebrews: 1825 2nd Edition

Book of Mormon Authors: Their Words and Messages

Prophet of the Jubilee

Manuscript Found: The Complete Original "Spaulding Manuscript"

Latter-day Saint Social Life: Social Research on the LDS Church and Its Members

From Jerusalem to Zarahemla: Literary and Historical Studies of the Book of Mormon

Religion, Mental Health, and the Latter-day Saints

Zion's Trumpet: 1849 Welsh Mormon Periodical

Things of Redeeming Worth: Scriptural Messages and World Judgments

## OCCASIONAL PAPERS SERIES

Excavations at Seila, Egypt

## OTHER

Christopher Columbus: A Latter-day Saint Perspective

Church History in Black and White: George Edward Anderson's Photographic Mission to Latter-day Saint Historical Sites

California Saints: A 150-Year Legacy in the Golden State

A Woman's View: Helen Mar Whitney's Reminiscences of Early Church History

Joseph Smith Portraits: A Search for the Prophet's Likeness

A Descriptive Bibliography of the Mormon Church

Brigham Young: Images of a Mormon Prophet

Prophets and Apostles of the Last Dispensation

The Restored Gospel and the Message of the Four Gospels

# THINGS OF
# REDEEMING
# WORTH

—⧟⧟—

## *Scriptural Messages and World Judgments*

### H. Curtis Wright

Volume Sixteen
in the Religious Studies Center
Specialized Monograph Series

**RELIGIOUS STUDIES CENTER**
BRIGHAM YOUNG UNIVERSITY

**Library of Congress Cataloging-in-Publication Data**

Wright, H. Curtis (Herbert Curtis), 1928–
    Things of redeeming worth : scriptural messages and world
judgments / H. Curtis Wright.
        p.        cm.
    Includes bibliographical references.
    ISBN 1-57008-745-8 (alk. paper)
    1. Church of Jesus Christ of Latter-day Saints—Doctrines.    I. Title.

BX8637 .W75  2002
230'.9332—dc21                                                          2001008431

Printed in the United States of America                    54459-6865
Malloy Lithographing Incorporated, Ann Arbor, MI

10   9    8    7    6    5    4    3    2    1

Distributed by
Deseret Book Company
Salt Lake City, Utah

# DEDICATED IN THE NAME OF THE LORD

To *Nephi*, for words like these:

> "Behold he cometh . . .
> [into the world]. And the world,
> because of their iniquity
> shall judge him to be a thing of naught;
> wherefore they scourge him,
> and he suffereth it; and they smite him, and
> he suffereth it. Yea, they spit
> upon him, and he suffereth it,
> because of his loving kindness and
> his long-suffering towards
> the children of men"
> (1 Ne. 19:8–9).

> "Wo unto them that turn aside the just [one] for
> a thing of naught and revile against
> that which is good, and say
> that it is of no worth!"
> (2 Ne. 28:16; cf. 2 Ne. 27:29–32).

> "There are many
> that harden their hearts
> against the Holy Spirit, that
> it hath no place in them;
> wherefore, they cast many things
> away . . . and esteem them
> as things of naught"
> (2 Ne. 33:2).

To *Jeannene Dowding Wright* (d. 1996), wife of my youth and mother of my children;

And to *Jeanne Bates Wright*, wife of my retirement and old age.

# Contents

# Introduction

# Rejection of the Recency Fetish

Modern science constitutes a religion of matter and energy that studies particles in motion, and nothing else. Its worldview, which governs propositions about the natural order and everything in it, is dominated by "presentism" because its origin in sensory observations of physical phenomena precludes inclusion of anything people of normal sensory and intellectual abilities cannot detect by means of their senses.[1] Since phenomena are observable only in the present, however, no one can observe the phenomena of yesterday or tomorrow, which must be reconstructed through messages and artifacts from the past or predicted from observations in present time that are always subject to change; and "since the method of science is observation . . . there is very little that we can ascertain about the mind," or about anything else that cannot be observed, "by following the method of science."[2]

The present, accordingly, is the only legitimate province of science, which seeks empirical certitude through the accurate communication of human sensory experience. But we are "stuck" with our own sensory experiences and cannot experience the sensations of others. It is therefore impossible for human beings to communicate their sensations, which are always private, personal, unique, individual, and absolutely nontransferable. So you have your sensations, I have mine, and never the twain shall match — which means (1) that we can only communicate information *about* our sensations; (2) that empirical truth is relative to its cultural milieu; (3) that science cannot reveal the absolute truth about anything; and (4) that scientists must ultimately settle for eliminating error from propositions about the observable universe. That, to shorten a lengthy story, is what scientists do: they eliminate as much error as possible from propositions about the only world knowable to science. But science does not—indeed *cannot*—say anything at all about any other world than this one.

These four essays betray my objections to the confining presentism of the recency fetish imposed by the precipitous rise and spurious impact of scientific thinking on every aspect of modern life. I share Whitehead's objections to the monkey-see-monkey-do etiquette of our academic institutions, which stems from the success of early physics, the first science to be systematized in modern times. But chemistry, the first science to be modeled on physics, was also "the *last* success of materialistic thought," according to Whitehead, that "has not ultimately proved to be double-edged,"[3] for modern thought has developed in strict simian fashion. "The prestige of the more scientific form," he says, "belongs to the physical sciences," which lead directly to the social sciences and indirectly to the humanities and fine arts because "biology apes the manners of physics"[4]—just as physiology apes the manners of biology, psychology apes the manners of physiology, and the social sciences that ape psychology also ape each other and other ologies all the way back to physics.[5] I object to this *religio scientiae* and its glorification of temporal data, empirical methods, and the present moment. I also object to its insistence on learning by study and its exclusion of learning by faith. I categorically reject, furthermore, the powerful ancient-to-modern sophism of humanly originated science as an all-inclusive *everythingology* that makes it impossible to consider anything *sub specie aeternitatis*. Science, to me, is like Popeye: it is what it is, and that's *all* that it is; and it is assuredly not the study of all that is. My justification for combining essays on things of redeeming worth written in the late fifties, early eighties, and middle nineties is thus twofold: first, that modern secular thinking, like its ancient and medieval antecedents, is wholly nonredemptive; and second, that all of these essays, by regarding the redemption of human beings from an eternal perspective, address the basic themes of human life and salvation that are not novel and do not change.

These essays, accordingly, are not about the humanistic religion of personal merit that offers salvation only to those who "earn" it through scrupulous commandment-keeping and the faithful performance of ordinances. They are about the revealed religion of vicarious merit, which offers forgiveness and rebirth only to those who have sufficient faith in Christ to humble themselves before God and repent of all personal sinfulness. I have witnessed, and continue to witness, both kinds of religion in The Church of Jesus Christ of Latter-day Saints; but I have rejected the former, which I absorbed like a sponge or a vacuum cleaner from youthful activity in the Church, and accepted the latter, which I discovered in the Book of Mormon as a U.S. Navy airman second class.

I didn't like military life; but it blessed me anyway, for when I rejected the allurements of shore leave in the forties, it triggered my first intense exposure to the Book of Mormon. And forthwith, on my bunk in the barracks of a naval air station, I learned that I had two religions: the religion of my youth, which — in spite of its activities, hundred-percent awards, and seminary classes — was all church and no gospel; and religion in the Book of Mormon, where the Church was founded squarely upon the gospel or it was not Christ's Church. I also learned, as an unconverted Latter-day Saint, that I had confused the superstructure with the foundation of revealed religion and built its basement on top of its house. On learning all this, as might be expected, I went through the *Sturm und Drang* of evaluating my humanistic religion of personal merit — of faith in my own ability to obey moral laws and perform ritual requirements *perfectly* — against my redemptive religion of faith in the merits of Christ. In the end, to sum everything up, it was no contest, for I abandoned the former, accepted the latter, and made no bones about it. Since then, needless to say, my life has never been, and *deo volente* can never be, the same.

I have not always accepted the Book of Mormon as the doctrinal standard of the Restoration; but I do now. The strongest convictions and innermost feelings of my *revealed witness* about it are best expressed, perhaps, in the words of a civil engineer, who, after long years of teaching revealed religion by the Spirit of the Lord at BYU, said to me: "I shudder to think what might have become of me — where I might be today, and what I might be doing right now — if I had never run into the Book of Mormon!" All of these essays echo that sentiment by suggesting that Latter-day Saints should be wary of any religious dictum based on the false assumptions of personal merit, which stem directly from the agonistic ideal of competitive excellence on the Homeric battlefield and its secular legacy of sophic spirituality to Western civilization. It therefore goes without saying that I no longer believe in justification by personal merit, the false doctrine that deceives us into thinking we can "earn" the favor of God by amassing our own self-accumulated treasuries of "good works." Thus, we must differentiate that unholy belief from the true doctrine of justification by vicarious merit— the doctrine that God forgives personal sinfulness *only* through personal faith in the merits of Jesus Christ. We must also distinguish between justification by the grace of God through faith in the Atonement of Jesus Christ and the twin necessities of justification by law and governance by law.

## Justification by Grace through Faith

Justification is a scriptural term for the forgiven status of anyone who is vindicated or acquitted of all sin and approved in the eyes of God. When people are justified, accordingly, they are forgiven by God, who looks upon them as though they were righteous individuals who had never sinned. Those who would understand the scriptural doctrine of justification must therefore discover how people arrive at this state of acceptance by the Father, or, in other words, how they acquire this grace, benevolence, or favor with God.

In latter-day revelation, as in the teachings of Paul, the only basis for man's acceptance by the Father is faith in the Atonement of Christ. It is worth noting, in this connection, that there is no such thing as abstract faith. The first principle of the gospel, be it noted, is not simply faith: it is *faith in the Lord Jesus Christ*. Faith can never be faith in nothing, for all faith must have a repository; and in all of the scriptures, justification is based not on faith in *anything* but on faith in Christ. The idea of absolute and unqualified acceptance of something is implicit in the word "faith," and the thing that must be accepted unequivocally is the mediation and Atonement of Jesus Christ. Without this redeeming faith in his Son, we are told, it is impossible for anyone to please the Father (see Heb. 11:6), by which we understand that we must be won over to Christ, convinced—intellectually, emotionally, and in every other way— that he alone can provide our only means of worshiping the Father acceptably. We cannot therefore be justified by God unless our faith, our trust, and our confidence are in Christ, who suffered, bled, and died for us.

The Book of Mormon supports Paul's rejection of the false belief that justification is based on obedience to ritual, moral, or natural law (see 2 Ne. 2:5; 25:23–29; Mosiah 12:27–32; 13:27–33; 15:19; 16:13–15). In order to understand its attitudes toward law, however, the concepts of justification by faith and by law must be disentangled. While Paul and others clearly insist that those who have no faith in Christ cannot be *justified* by law, they make it equally clear that those who are justified by faith in Christ are also *governed* by law. There is thus a compelling distinction between *being justified by law*, which is abjectly impossible, and *being governed by law*, which is inevitable because all kingdoms have laws their inhabitants must abide or they cannot live in them.

## Justification by Law

Sin is defined in scripture as the breaking of law. Thus, all who sin by breaking any of the laws of God fall "under the curse of a broken law" (Moro. 8:24) and are liable to the punishments affixed by justice for their sins. Since God is just, moreover, and cannot make allowances for sin (see Alma 45:16; D&C 1:31), they will be punished, not only by their sins in this life but for their sins in the day of judgment, *unless* the Atonement intervenes and pays the penalty of their sinning for them, in which case they will not suffer for their sins. If there were anyone on earth who had never sinned, anyone who had rendered perfect obedience to every law of God, that person would be justified by God solely on the basis of obedience to law. But Paul warns that those who expect to be justified by law are debtors to do the whole law, to render absolutely perfect obedience to every law of God all the time; and James says that anyone who offends in one little point of the law is guilty of breaking the whole law (see James 2:10; see also Gal. 3:10; 5:1–3). We must therefore conclude, inasmuch as all have sinned and are subject to the penalties imposed by justice for their sins, that we cannot be justified by God on the basis of our imperfect obedience to his perfect laws, regardless of how "good" we may appear to be in the eyes of men. It may be said that Christ is the one and only person in human history, past, present, or future, who is justified by law in the sight of God, and this because he is the one and only sinless man—sinless "because he was the

Son of God, and had the fulness of the Spirit, and greater power than any man."[6]

## Governance by Law

The idea that believers in Christ have no obligation to the laws of God is as foreign to scripture as the notion that people are accepted by the Father on the basis of their own merits without having faith in the Atonement of his Son. The prophets speak consistently of "good works" as those doings, actions, or performances of believers which are inspired and motivated by faith in Christ, dedicated to keeping his commandments, and directed toward building up his kingdom. These are, in their thinking, the only truly "good" works. When prophets tell people to work out their own salvation (see Philip. 2:12; Alma 34:37; Morm. 9:27), for example, they are not encouraging humanists to merit salvation by their works: they are exhorting those who already believe in God to come unto Christ, observe the laws and commandments of his Father, and produce the good works that always result from but never cause their faith.

The Book of Mormon, as a matter of fact, condemns the secular doctrine of personal merit, and is supported in this condemnation by the Doctrine and Covenants and the Prophet Joseph Smith (see 2 Ne. 2:8; 31:19–20; Mosiah 2:19; Alma 22:14; 24:10; Hel. 14:13; Moro. 6:4; D&C 3:20).[7] Thus, we can't even get through the gate or onto the path that leads to eternal life, according to Nephi, "save it were by the word of Christ with unshaken faith in him, relying *wholly* upon the merits of him who is mighty to save" (2 Ne. 31:19; emphasis added). Alma adds that "since man had fallen he could not merit *anything* of himself" because it is "the sufferings and death of Christ" that bring redemption to all who accept the gospel by atoning "for their sins, through faith and repentance, and so forth" (Alma 22:14; emphasis added). And Moroni concludes that we, like the Nephites, must be "continually watchful unto prayer, relying *alone* upon the merits of Christ, who was the author and the finisher of their faith" (Moro. 6:4; emphasis added). That leaves us with no excuse for relying upon our own merits as a means of obtaining salvation. Redemption is thus an invasion of our world by the power of God's world, for as Paul tells Titus, it is "the grace of God that bringeth salvation" into the natural order, where it "hath appeared to all men" (Titus 2:11). One of Paul's faithful sayings, moreover, instructs Titus to "affirm constantly, that they which have believed in God might be careful to maintain good works. . . . And let our people also learn to maintain good works for necessary uses, that they be not unfruitful" (Titus 3:8, 14). This counsel agrees perfectly with Alma's advice to the Nephites: "See that ye have faith, hope, and charity, and *then* ye will always abound in good works" (Alma 7:24; emphasis added)—it is definitely not the other way around. The point is therefore clear: without faith in Christ we cannot be justified by obedience to law or by good works because our obedience is imperfect and our works are meritorious only in the sight of men; and conversely, believers who repent of their sins and are justified by faith in Christ must, as Paul says, bear fruit and maintain good works. Thus, believers are never relieved of responsibility to the laws of God, even though they do not expect to be justified by them: they are required to keep God's commandments as best they can, with adequate provision through the Atonement for repentance and forgiveness when they fail (see 1 Jn. 2:1-2; Mosiah 26:30). Those who lack faith in Christ, on the other hand, cannot be redeemed by keeping God's commandments, whereas those who have faith in him are required to do so; and the redeemed are those authentic believers in Christ who rejoice in his Father's forgiveness of their sins because they are *justified* by his grace through faith in the grace of his Son (see D&C 20:30-31) and *governed* by the laws of his kingdom.

That, I think, summarizes the theological "jist" of all these essays.

## Notes

1. This scientific limitation obtains even if scientists employ sophisticated artificial instruments, which must themselves be observable and are often untrustworthy, in order to enhance the natural abilities of their own human senses.

2. C. E. M. Joad, *Philosophy for Our Times* (New York: Thomas Nelson and Sons, 1940), 107. On the scientific reduction of psychology to somatology through observationalism, see ibid., 104-26.

3. Alfred North Whitehead, *Science and the Modern World*, Lowell Lectures, 1925 (New York: Macmillan, 1962), 87.

4. Ibid., 150. For further discussion, see "Whitehead's Criticism of Science" in my article "Science and the Institutional Professions," *Scholar and Educator* (spring 1982): 11–15.

5. Dehumanization also characterizes the humanities and fine arts, where "the reactions of science have so far been unfortunate" because "its materialistic basis has [also] directed attention to *things* as opposed to *values*" in aesthetic fields; ibid., 291, 293. "Even naturalistic *art*," says Whitehead, "is more akin to the practice of physics, chemistry, and biology than is the practice of law" and similar institutional professions; ibid., 280–81.

6. *Teachings of the Prophet Joseph Smith*, comp. Joseph Fielding Smith (Salt Lake City: Deseret Book, 1938), 187–88.

7. Ibid., 58.

# A Thing of Naught:
# World Judgment and
# The Trial of Jesus Christ

*In the Gospel of Matthew we read an account of a lawyer who asked Jesus a question and tempted him, saying, "Master, which is the great commandment in the law?" We are familiar with the answer of the Savior: "Thou shalt love the Lord thy God with all thy heart, and with all thy soul, and with all thy mind. This is the first and great commandment. And the second is like unto it, Thou shalt love thy neighbour as thyself." Perhaps not as many realize that Jesus turned interrogator and asked those gathered this question, "What think ye of Christ? whose son is he?" (Matt. 22:37–39, 42). This question has been echoed whenever men have been confronted with the message of Christianity.*

*In our modern world some dismiss Jesus as merely an ethical and moral teacher of righteousness. Others think of Jesus as symbolic, originating from a mythological point of view. To them, he is not the resurrected Christ, the literal Son of God, but merely a man in whom tradition and myths have been catapulted into a place of prominence. Some would deny not only the historical Jesus but would shun his way of life with regards to ethics and morality.*

*A few accept and understand Jesus as the living Christ, the Son of God, in whom all life is centered. He is "the way, the truth, and the life" (John 14:6), "for there is none other name under heaven given among men, whereby we must be saved" (Acts 4:12). Salvation is not only redemption from physical death but from spiritual death. He redeems people from the effects of the Fall and will cleanse them from their sins if they have faith in Christ and repent. But others are confused and bewildered when confronted with the concept of the Christ and the message of Jesus.*

*Curtis Wright's pamphlet "A Thing of Naught" brings into sharp focus the mission of the Savior. He utilizes the trial of Jesus to indicate how people respond to the Savior. It is an interesting treatment of how men will handle the question, "What think ye of Christ?" This pamphlet should be helpful to every thoughtful person who desires to understand the message of Christianity in the midst of a confused world.*

*B. West Belnap*
*Dean of Religious Instruction, 1962–66*
*Brigham Young University*

For many years now I have been deeply interested in the trial of Jesus. It all began in seminary when I saw a film presentation of that trial, which left a vivid and permanent impression upon me. The scene I remember best showed Christ among the soldiers. He was sitting in the barracks clothed in Herod's robe, and the soldiers were amusing themselves at his expense. Earlier in the trial he had claimed to be a king; and so they had put him on a "throne," dressed him in "royal purple," and placed a reed in his hand representing the scepter of his "sovereignty."

The climax of their sport occurred when the soldiers decided to make a "crown" for their king. After a wreath had been hurriedly plaited out of thorns, it was placed upon a pillow and brought before him. And while the soldiers stood about in squadrons, heads bowed in mocking reverence, one of their number removed the thorny diadem and "crowned" the king. Immediately the shout went up, "Hail! King of the Jews! Hail! King of the Jews!" In the confusion that followed, the soldiers thronged the Savior, striking him with their hands and bowing before him in mock worship; and against this raucous backdrop the camera kept moving closer and closer to Jesus, until, in a final close-up of his face, tiny rivulets of blood could be seen trickling down his forehead and onto his cheek.

I remember thinking as I watched the trial of Jesus that God was saying something really basic about us. Chronology was all mixed up. It was not as though he were accusing the soldiers who had mocked the Lord or Judas who had betrayed him, or Peter who had denied him, or the apostles who had all forsaken him and fled, or even Caiaphas and the Sanhedrin who had condemned him without hearing his defense, or Pilate who had

WHAT TO DO WITH JESUS?

Like Pilate — A question we all must answer.

Printed in the **Deseret News** on Friday, April 11, 1952. Used by permission.

written the execution order, or Herod who had "set him at nought." There was more to it than that. The implications of that trial were important enough to transcend the limitations of time and place. God was speaking to us. He was pointing to a universal tendency in human nature, something that expressed itself again and again in every generation; and in a very real sense, we were being indicted by the trial of Jesus Christ.

Now it is not surprising that many of our commentators completely miss that aspect of the trial. After all, the Savior hinted that there were "hidden" messages in the scriptures when he said that only those with ears to hear and eyes to see would understand. This meant that many would look without seeing and listen without hearing. And the danger of overlooking these hidden messages is especially acute in this modern age of experts. We have amassed concentrated studies on specialized subject matters by the top men in virtually every field of knowledge, but we feel at the same time that we are sacrificing breadth for depth. Our theology, for example, is extremely detailed and in some ways very accurate. But how meaningful is it? In our modern preoccupation with analysis we are able to understand the individual parts all right, but the more general features which build the parts into a unified and meaningful whole elude us. This predilection for hyperanalysis is aptly described by a simple analogy.

> You may recall from your childhood those picture puzzles which frequently appeared in magazines. Maybe they still fascinate you. There was one that taught a great lesson. It was a picture of a little boy beside a big tree in a deep forest. In the far background was a house that looked very small in the distance. Beneath the picture were these words: "This little boy is lost. He is looking for his father, who is very near to him, but he cannot find him. Can you find the boy's father in the picture?" That was the puzzle. And, indeed, it certainly was a puzzle! You examined the picture from every point of view, turning it first one way and then another. You held it close, searched every corner, and even turned it upside down. But the father was nowhere to be found. Finally you put it aside in defeat. After a while you happened to glance at the picture there on the table where you left it, and suddenly you saw from a distance the clear outline of the father. You wondered how you could have missed him, for now you could see nothing else. The curves of the skyline formed his head and shoulders, the branches of the trees outlined his body, and the tree trunks made his legs. He was so big in proportion to the boy, and the house, and everything else in the picture. That's why you missed him at first. You were not looking for one so big.[1]

It is difficult to avoid the conclusion nowadays that something like that has happened to biblical scholarship. Many of our theologians are so concerned with analyzing details that they can't see the general picture of anything. They are very proficient in examining the historical and literary problems of the Bible, but they seem to miss its general message of salvation. Everyone wants to study that particular part of the Bible which coincides with his subject specialty. The trial of Jesus, for example, has a tremendous appeal to specialists in the legal profession. A quick check of holdings in any good library will turn up at least a dozen writers of this type who have published whole books on the subject, including some multivolume works. Their approach, generally speaking, has been similar to that of the lawyer George W. Thompson, whose interest in the "legal aspects" of the trial of Jesus led to a rigorous investigation of Hebrew and Roman jurisprudence, against which his findings as to the legality of the trial and verdict were presented in an exhaustive study. Titles of such works include *The Trial of Jesus from a Lawyer's Standpoint; The Case of the Nazarene Reopened; The Prosecution of Jesus, Its Date, History and Legality; The Illegality of the Trial of Jesus; The Legality of the Trial of Jesus; The Trial of Jesus Christ, a Legal Monograph; The Trial of Jesus, a Judicial Review of the Law and Facts of the World's Most Tragic Courtroom Trial;* and *A Lawyer Reviews the Illegal Trial of Jesus.*[2] The injustices of the Jewish and Roman courts receive the emphasis in most of these monographs, while the more general moral and theological considerations tend to be minimized, if they are treated at all. These *magna opera* with their comprehensive coverage, meticulous footnotes, and lengthy bibliographies impress us with the assurance that we have mastered the obscure legal minutiae of the trial, but they also remind us that we have largely missed the point. We have spent a lot of time and research on the Savior's trial, but the basic implications of that trial for our own generation have escaped us.

The most significant commentaries on the trial of Jesus Christ are found, of all places, in the Book of Mormon. That trial was witnessed by Nephi hundreds of years before it happened when it was shown to him in a vision by an angel from God. He saw the significance of that trial and summarized it in these words: "And it came to pass that the angel spake unto me again, saying: Look! And I looked and beheld the Lamb of God, that he was taken by the people; yea, the Son of the everlasting God was judged of the world; and I saw and bear record. And I, Nephi, saw that he was lifted up upon the cross and slain for the sins of the world" (1 Ne. 11:32–33).

Now, Latter-day Saints, at least, would do well to consider the serious implications of those remarks. Nephi apparently looked upon that trial as an expression of *world* judgment. He did not connect it directly with the judicial practices of the first century. According to him the Savior was taken by *the people*, not just by Judas and his band; furthermore, he was brought into a *world* courtroom, not merely into the Jewish and Roman courts; and there he was judged *of the world*, not of Caiaphas, or Herod, or Annas, or Pontius Pilate. And when he was finally condemned and "lifted up upon the cross and slain," it was "for the sins of the world," not for the crimes of blasphemy or sedition. These are solemn thoughts, and this is a serious indictment on the part of Nephi. He is saying that Jesus died for the same world which condemned him, and he means to accuse *all* of us—the whole world—of complicity in the trial of Jesus!

And there is more truth than fiction in that accusation. We know that a man's personal estimate of Jesus Christ determines his own judgment in the eyes of God. Men are free, of course, to form their own opinions about the Savior; but they are also accountable for those opinions. It is obvious, however, that we differ widely in our evaluations of him. In the judgment of some, including many "important" people, he is worth nothing—zero! To others, the worth of his atoning life and death, the price for which he bought us, is beyond all comprehension of value. Our world, like that of other generations, is sharply divided on this issue. In the words of Nephi: "The things which some men esteem to be of great worth, both to the body and soul, others set at naught and trample under their feet. Yea, even the very God of Israel do men trample under their feet; . . . they set him at naught, and hearken not to the voice of his counsels" (1 Ne. 19:7).

This idea of world judgment, implicit in the trial of Jesus, was later repeated and reaffirmed by Nephi: "And *the world*, because of their iniquity, shall judge him to be a thing of naught; wherefore *they* scourge him, and he suffereth it; and *they* smite him, and he suffereth it. Yea, *they* spit upon him, and he suffereth it, because of his loving kindness and his long-suffering towards the children of men. And the God of our fathers ... yieldeth himself ... as a man, into the hands of wicked men, to be lifted up, ... and to be crucified, ... and to be buried in a sepulchre" (1 Ne. 19:9–10; emphasis added).

Once more we note the far-reaching implications of Nephi's remarks. It was *the world* who judged him to be a thing of naught: they not only found him guilty, but worthless. They had a good reason, of course, for bringing in that verdict. Jesus had exposed their iniquities by testifying of their sins, and so they had officially condemned him in their courts, intending to silence him forever, as though he were the sinner for saying such things about them (cf. Hel. 13:24–28). It was *the world,* furthermore, who scourged him and smote him and spat upon him. Nephi insists that *the world* is the culprit: *they* did it. He will not let us escape responsibility by blaming Pontius Pilate and the Jews, for he knows that our iniquities prompt us to make the same judgments they made; and that is especially true when the Savior exposes our iniquities, as he did theirs. It is only when we confess those iniquities and humble ourselves before God, seeking forgiveness in repentance, that we are acquitted of complicity in the trial of Jesus. The truth hurts, they say, and that is verily true of this truth. But only in its light can we see the Savior as he really is; and only when we see him as he really is can we sense the infinite worth of his Atonement and the high cost of our redemption through his sufferings and the shedding of his blood.

The world has never seen things that way, and it never will. In every age those who have really believed in the infinite worth of Christ's Atonement have been a definite minority. Even the few who have held this view of things have not always held it: they have had to *come* to it, sometimes through a brutal and agonizing process of reorientation in which they finally got their thinking straight about religion. But meanwhile, the masses of men have gone right on making the age-old mistakes of Pontius Pilate and the Sanhedrin. There's no doubt about it. Nephi's observations will hold up in any age. The trial of Jesus Christ confronts us with a world picture that portrays a great deal about us and about our generation.

Nevertheless, we can't help wondering what prompted Nephi to interpret the trial in typological terms. In doing so he obviously extended its meaning far beyond the immediate context of the first century and the literal statements of the New Testament. But why did he do that? Well, we learn from the Book of Mormon that he lived in a world of "signs, and wonders, and types, and shadows" which were based invariably on the redemption, the grand, underlying theme of all true religion. He lived in a time of great expectation when the minds of the people were continually looking forward to the promised coming of the Son of God. There was among the ancients a vast and uniform system of similitudes and types which formed an integral part of the prophetic method in both hemispheres.[3] These ubiquitous types were based on revelation from God and designed by him to assist men in coming to Christ and repenting of their sins. They appeared in history and prophecy and were the foundation and superstructure of all ritual, where they served as supplements to worship. They were effective only because of their direct association with the Atonement of Jesus Christ, the primitive theme of all Nephi's theology. Here are a few expressions of that theme:

> My soul delighteth in the scriptures, and my heart pondereth them, and writeth them for the learning and the profit of my children. Behold, my soul delighteth in the things of the Lord; and my heart pondereth continually upon the things which I have seen and heard (2 Ne. 4:15–16).

> Behold, my soul delighteth in proving unto my people the truth of the coming of Christ; for, for this end hath the law of Moses been given; and *all things which have been given of God from the beginning of the world, unto man, are the typifying of him....* And my soul delighteth in proving unto my people that save Christ should come all men must perish (2 Ne. 11:4, 6; emphasis added).

> For we labor diligently to write, to persuade our children, and also our brethren, to believe in Christ, and to be reconciled to God; ... And we talk of Christ, we rejoice in Christ, we preach of Christ, we prophesy of Christ, and we write according to our prophecies, that our children may know to what source they may look for a remission of their sins (2 Ne. 25:23, 26).

That goes a long way toward explaining Nephi's sweeping statements about the trial and world judgment. It is one of those revealing types and shadows of which he spoke so often. That does not minimize its historical actuality or its literal implications: it merely extends its application to the world in all its generations. God actually intended that the trial be typical in nature and that it carry a rebuke to the world for its typical judgment of his Only Begotten Son.

Another statement by Nephi helps us understand further his typological orientation and his attitude toward scripture. "I did read many things to them [my brethren] . . . which were written in the books of Moses; but that I might more fully persuade them to believe in the Lord their Redeemer I did read unto them that which was written by the prophet Isaiah; *for I did liken all scriptures unto us, that it might be for our profit and learning*" (1 Ne. 19:22–23; emphasis added).

Well, that's simple enough, isn't it? Nephi's approach to the word of God was *so* simple, as a matter of fact, that we never would have guessed it. He merely related the ancient scriptures to modern contemporary situations among his own people. That was possible, of course, only because the scriptures have from the beginning treated the great basic themes of life and experience. If more of those who preach religion would only realize that, they wouldn't complain so bitterly about the sagging interest of their yawning congregations. Nephi's people were probably amazed to find that human nature hadn't changed very much since it was created. It was only the situations that changed, as though the same old picture were given a new frame now and then. The scriptures always reminded them of themselves or someone they knew just down the street. That's why they profited so greatly from the word of God and why they learned so much from studying it. Those old books came alive for Nephi's listeners. They met real flesh-and-blood people in the scriptures, people with problems and hopes and fears just like their own. There were good and bad examples among them, to be sure, and they found plenty of mysteries incapable of scientific proof. There were even some embarrassing passages about sex in which the extreme depravity of sinners was revealed; and the critics probably said those old texts were unreliable and could not be trusted. But through it all the faith of the fathers was somehow transmitted to the children, and a knowledge of the Son of God increased among the sons of men, at least among the faithful. But I fear that we will never thrill with that exhilarating experience of reading the scriptures as long as we regard ancient history as though it never really happened. And while our modern preachers continue to treat the word of God as the mythological product of day-before-yesterday, their congregations will continue to become the audiences of play-wrights and actors who treat the word of man as the factual product of today, for fact presented as fiction can never hope to compete with fiction presented as fact—especially when it sounds like it came from the dank and musty swamps of ten thousand years ago! The former is verily worse than the latter.

And now . . . suddenly, those remarks about world judgment begin to make sense. Nephi is suggesting that we follow his example and liken the trial of Jesus unto ourselves so we can learn something from it that might profit us; and somehow that doesn't seem like a bad idea anymore. It shouldn't bother us overmuch to find that our more critical theologians disagree with Nephi. They prefer what they call their "historico-critical method" because they exalt learning by study over learning by faith. They never cease their tireless evaluation of other men's works, although they produce very little themselves, and *it* is not flawless, by any means. They are fond of reviewing an opus by pointing out its historical inaccuracies, internal inconsistencies, chronological anachronisms and stylistic limitations; and they are especially critical of an author's way of thinking. Some of them go so far as to rule out the whole realm of typology. They would maintain that there is nothing in the scriptures to justify Nephi's extra-literal interpretation of the trial. He was just being overly enthusiastic in reporting what he saw in that vision. Isn't it easier to believe that he was simply overstating the facts? He was reading something into the trial, something that wasn't there at all. But then most scriptural writers use hyperbole occasionally: its one of their favorite tricks. Nephi needn't be embarrassed because they caught him at it. All this assumes, you understand, that he actually *saw* a vision; he *could* have invented that too: that would have been easy to do, especially if Joseph Smith invented him in the first place! And there is nothing in the New Testament to support his wild contention that the *world* prosecuted Jesus. It was a handful of religious fanatics who did it. Oh, of course, they were clever enough to implicate others in their designs. They used a mob and a Roman governor, for example, to accomplish the death of their victim. But strictly speaking, *they* were responsible for the deed. Nephi is overdoing it when he insists that the world must share in their guilt. The very most we can say is that the Jewish nation and the Roman government collaborated to form a conspiracy against the Savior, and even that exaggerates the facts. No, it was not the world that condemned the Lord as Nephi suggests—not even the world of the first century, to say nothing of its other generations.

But that particular kind of reasoning is rather patronizing, isn't it? It is precisely this devious worldly thinking that Nephi was talking about. He would have had great difficulty tolerating our shallow, superficial approach to everything and our condescending propensity for getting tangled up in technicalities. He meant what he said about world judgment, all right, even though he didn't expect the world, or worldly theologians for that matter, to agree with him. There was no room on those plates for the historico-critical nonsense that stuffs our theological journals; and the reasons for this are worth noting.

Nephi clearly foresaw that the modern quest of the historical Jesus would obscure the Christ of faith because there are two kinds of theology. *Revealed theology* explains the meaning of our presence in the natural universe through living witnesses that come to us from God's presence in another universe. All explanations of *systematic theology*, however, are humanly originated formulations based on critical studies of recorded scripture and historical tradition. Nephi understood, to be sure, that we need explanations — but *not* by speculation. What we need most, since God alone is wise, is *actual* revelation: historic revelation, important as it is, cannot redeem us; and there is no salvation in the human speculations of systematic theology. There is, of course, no essential conflict between systematic theology and history because both studies are humanly originated and neither study is governed by supernatural assumptions. In a revealed religion, on the other hand, conflict with the secular outlook of the human arts and of the scientific, philosophical, and historical disciplines is inevitable, since revealed information is not derived from the natural order by the reasoned speculations of human wisdom: it is brought into the natural order by informed messengers from another world order who know whereof they speak because they come directly from the presence of God. The ultimate realities of revealed religion therefore lie completely beyond history, not within it. History can *clarify* religious experience but can neither determine nor authenticate it. The gospel is thus an intrusion into this world from outside, an invasion of nature by the grace of God in which human wisdom is subordinate to the wisdom of God; it is not the secular worship of human wisdom in which the mind of God is subordinated to the mind of man, as in the historical determinism of systematic theology.[4]

Nephi, accordingly, recorded only those things which were pleasing to God and to those who were *not* of this world. His words contain an implicit warning against swallowing whole-cloth the bland, predigested conclusions of professional theologians who want to spare us the agony of thinking for ourselves. He would rebuke us, furthermore, for jumping wildly to conclusions based on our first hasty perusal of the sources. He would send us back again to those same sources in the hope of inspiring some second thoughts. And if we would only stop telling ourselves that we know it all long enough to listen to him for a moment, we might learn something. And then, perhaps, we would humble ourselves and go back to the New Testament in order to reread its accounts of the trial in the light of this world's attitudes toward Jesus Christ.

To begin with, the conspiracy against Jesus was inspired by the religious motives of pious public officials whose sense of virtue had been outraged.[5] We must disagree with the bulk of Christian writers who describe the leaders of the Jews as hoodlums and outlaws, rascals and ruffians, rogues and scoundrels, knaves and villains, or blackguards and highwaymen of the deepest, darkest hue. That, I'm afraid, really *is* a "magnificent hyperbole" and a gross distortion of the truth. They were criminals all right, but of a vastly different piece. They had no use for the seamy side of crime and campaigned relentlessly against it. They were not unprincipled hoodlums lurking in the black recesses of unlighted cities and slinking through dark alleys. No, indeed! For they didn't like darkness — or dirt! They moved in the upper strata of Jewish high society and lived in the better sections of Jerusalem; and they bathed every day. They inhabited the country club ionosphere of the city's "velvet alleys" where they breathed the rarefied air of religious piety and unimpeachable integrity. Nor were they like Chicago gangsters in the 1930s: they didn't have an arsenal where they stashed tommy guns and blackjacks and knives and rubber hoses and tear gas and brass knuckles and sawed-off shotguns and vials of nitroglycerin and acid and various poisons, both slow and fast acting; and there were no strong-arm methods, no bodies falling out of closets, no corpses floating down the river. Unlike our soldiers of World War II, they didn't know eighteen ways to kill a man, twelve of which were silent. But their legal methods were just as effective. And there were no handkerchiefs over their faces, no gloves to cover their fingerprints. They wore instead the robes of righteousness, the cloak of respectability and public trust, and the mantle of high official office. And in addition to that, they were exceptionally well educated. They were full of high-minded talk about the search for truth and the evils of ignorance. But meanwhile, they went efficiently about their business, unnoticed by the public at large. They operated in broad daylight, too, in full view of the law. They knew and insisted upon their rights, and they also knew how to "protect" them. They attempted to interpret and control the legal code, but they always stayed within its boundaries, for they were above all else respectable and irreproachable citizens.

Now spiritual wickedness has always had a way of ending up in high places; and just how that happens is described in detail, step by step, in the Nephite scriptures. "There are two great treatises on crime in the Book of Mormon, the one in Helaman, describing the doings of ancient Americans, the other in Mormon, describing the doings of modern Americans."[6] "It is organized crime and for the most part singularly respectable. Here we trace the general course of criminal doings . . . showing that the separate events and periods are not disconnected but represent a single great tradition. . . . Petty crime is no concern of the Book of Mormon, but rather wickedness in high places. The Book of Mormon tells us how such comes into existence and how it operates, and how it manages to surround itself with an aura of intense respectability and in time to legalize its evil practices,"[7] since "the criminal element is almost always large and usually predominant . . . and is always consciously and vocally on the side of virtue."[8]

The leaders of the Jews belong to that "single great tradition" of syndicated crime. It is an unbroken tradition that can be traced clearly all the way back to "that same being who did entice our first parents to partake of the forbidden fruit" (Hel. 6:26). The ways of the wicked are clearly disclosed by the Book of Mormon, and in the trial of Jesus the patterns of that ancient criminal tradition were followed almost to the letter by the conspirators — those suave, sophisticated zealots who were the respectable spiritual shepherds of Israel.

The plot against Jesus was an intricate and skillfully contrived project to get him out of the way. It was no jumbled mishmash of bungling schemes frantically hurled together at the last moment. It was instigated by the calm and reasoned planning of men with cool heads, who convened in secret and covenanted with one another to form a pact, and "took counsel together for to put him to death." They gathered at the swank city estate of Caiaphas, the high priest, and sat down together in the palatial mansion where they "consulted that they might take Jesus by [subtlety], and kill him" (Matt. 26:4; see also John 11:47–57; 12:19; and Luke 19:47–48; 22:1–2). It was a conspiracy in the worst sense of the term, and its perpetrators were the elite of Jerusalem, the impeccably reputable "men of affairs," the "solid citizens," the "chief priests, and the scribes, and the elders of the people." They recall vividly those earlier intrigues when, six hundred years before, the "Jews at Jerusalem," and later two of Lehi's own sons, had laid the groundwork for taking Lehi's life; and but for the intervention of the Lord who warned him of the danger in a dream, they would have succeeded.

> It was no excited street rabble or quick impulse of a city mob that threatened his life; certain parties "sought his life" (1 Ne. 1:20), with purpose and design. . . . The most significant thing about these plots is that their authors, "murderers in their hearts" (1 Ne. 17:44), had themselves convinced that they were doing the right thing; they believed that Lehi was a dangerous and irresponsible trouble maker, and in view of the international situation, treasonable and subversive to the bargain, while they themselves were defenders of respectability and the status quo. . . . Laman, Lemuel and the Jews at Jerusalem were defenders not only of common sense against a man "led away by the foolish imaginations of his heart" to exchange the comforts of gracious living for years of misery in the desert (1 Ne. 17:20), but they had solid conservative arguments of respectability and religion on their side. In daring to criticize them and to predict awful things about them, Lehi had set himself up as a judge.[9]

When that meeting was called and those men assembled from all parts of Jerusalem, the murderous processes of legalized assassination had long since been set in motion. The leaders of the Jews had probably begun whispering together early in the ministry of Jesus, shortly after he proclaimed himself as the Son of God. Had he alerted them already, as early as that wedding feast in Cana of Galilee? It was there at any rate that he first revealed himself publicly as the Messiah by turning water into wine. One thing is certain: there had been other meetings like this, lots of them, although they had been convoked as secretly as possible. But there were hints of the conspiracy all along—the way Jesus was treated in his home town; the repeated charges of sabbath breaking and demoniac possession; the murmurings and divisions he caused among the people; and the displeasure of the chief priests and scribes later on when the children shouted hosannas to him in the temple. And in spite of all the secrecy there are at least fifteen direct references to the conspiracy in the Gospels. Jesus knew about it, too, for he spoke of it many times himself in those cryptic passages about his death that so baffled his disciples. And we must not forget that the disgruntled Judas knew of the plot somehow, for he went willingly and directly to the conspirators to make a deal with them. They took him up on it, too. It turned out to be the worst deal he ever made in his life, for he sold his Savior and his soul for silver. That, as a matter of fact, is the worst bargain in the world, no matter how you look at it and no matter who makes it or when.

During that meeting the world's very finest criminal minds were at work. There they are, the reputable senior citizens of Jerusalem who really believe in the righteousness of their project. They include the best lawyers, of course, and important civic officials, as well as businessmen, educators, physicians, and prominent townspeople. And there is perfect unity among them. They are dedicated men, and they have assembled for a common purpose under the guidance and inspiration of their nation's responsible spiritual leaders. So here they are, in this meeting, conspiring together against Jesus. That describes their business perfectly, too, for "conspiring" really means "*breathing* together." And that's it. That's what they are doing. They are "breathing together" the real atmosphere of syndicated crime: the hot, stifling breath and sanctimonious talk of professional law-abiding criminals as they meet around the big walnut conference table of a stately west side manor for one of their planning sessions.

When that meeting was over the curtain began to descend on the earthly ministry of Jesus Christ. He sensed it, too, for on the same Tuesday afternoon while that criminal convocation was holding forth, he went with his disciples to the Mount of Olives where they also met in private. His words were especially sobering that day as he instructed the disciples about the end of the world and admonished them to prepare for it by telling stories of five foolish virgins and a man who hid his talent in the earth. He spoke also of the judgment to come, when all the nations would be gathered before the Son of Man. And he seemed to know of his own coming judgment when he would stand before the nations; for now, at the very moment when that other group was dispersing, he said plainly to his disciples, "Know ye that after two days is the feast of the passover, and the Son of man is betrayed to be crucified" (Matt. 26:1-2).[10] He knew all about the elaborate, imposing equipment of organized crime. The big shiny machine was well-oiled and running smoothly and all ready to go. Each component had been checked and double-checked and adjusted to a high degree of operating efficiency and integrated with the rest of the machine. All the bugs had been worked out by now, and there would be no mistakes. The lenses of the tracking mechanism were especially efficient: they had been ground and polished by experts; and they were now focused on him. From this point on that machine would trace his every move, until it finally moved in for the kill. He was in the crosshairs now. It had all begun to converge on him. In a few days he would be dead, legally and lawfully executed. He would be the victim, not of hoods and con men, but of professional conspirators; and their skirts would be "clean," for they were only irate citizens, campaigning in the name of justice and civic virtue and insisting on the protection of their rights! And let no one suppose, even for a moment, that they did not really believe in the righteousness of their crusade!

And his disciples just could not understand the reasons for that. It all seemed so abysmally tragic and pitiful to them. Their eyes were wet with weeping and full of heaviness. They could not yet see for sorrow that his crucifixion would be a triumph—not a tragedy, but a victory over the twin evils of death and sin. He had to go out of the world this way so that salvation could come into the world. That had been decreed in heaven before the world was and spoken by all the prophets from the beginning, and the scriptures had to be fulfilled. They could not yet understand that, but he knew they would understand it later on when he returned to them after his resurrection and endowed them with power from on high. So for the present, he did not explain it to them. He comforted them instead by speaking of the many mansions in his Father's house where he was going to prepare a place for them.

He also promised to come again and take them unto himself, that they might live with him in those mansions. And he prayed fervently for them, that they might be one with him as he was one with God.

On Thursday evening, the night of the grand performance in the garden, Judas played his part to perfection. His role was difficult, indeed: you might even say it was "treacherous" in places. But his evil nature had found its element, as though he had waited from all eternity for this one big scene. And when he kissed the Savior, he stole the entire show. The script called only for a kiss on the cheek as a means of identification. But according to the reviews of two reliable "critics" who were eyewitnesses to this drama, he put his whole being, his entire soul, into that kiss, fawning over the Lord in a moving portrayal of tenderness and warmth that feigned the deepest loyalty and devotion. The casting was superb, the presentation simply marvelous. Judas was a natural for the role of traitor. It was as though there had been real love in that kiss. No one could have done it better. Not even John the Beloved could have improved upon it.[11]

And it was no drunken street rabble that hauled Christ away from the garden, for that would have been illegal. He was officially arrested by "men and officers" sent by "the chief priests and elders" who represented "the people" in this case (see John 18:3 and Matt. 26:47). He was indeed "taken by the people" (1 Ne. 11:32), as Nephi said. The whole trial, in fact, could have been summarized on the dockets of the Jerusalem courts as "The People Against Jesus," for it was an aroused public conscience that considered him a dangerous nuisance and dealt with him accordingly.

After a brief appearance before Annas, he was bound over immediately to the Sanhedrin, the highest tribunal of the Jews. And how well that august body fits the patterns of organized crime! Like the Gadianton robbers, they filled the judgment seats, "employing their office very profitably indeed, 'letting the guilty and the wicked go unpunished because of their money;' and using their positions 'in office at the head of government . . . to get gain and glory'" (Hel. 7:5).[12] "Still, the judges had to proceed with some care, since they were supposed to be administering justice (Hel. 8:4), and could not be too crude and obvious in their attack, for even among the exceedingly wicked and depraved ... the feeling of civic virtue was perhaps as alive as it is in America today."[13]

They fumbled on the first play, for the false witnesses who were to perjure themselves under oath got their signals confused and were momentarily out of their places. But they quickly recovered the ball and started rolling again. A few plays later they scored a touchdown and found the prisoner guilty. All in all there were a few irregularities in the trial, but it satisfied the minimum requirements of the law and no one could accuse them of being underhanded about it.

They would have enjoyed executing him then and there, but there was a complication. Again like the Gadianton society, "these lawyers and judges had one annoying check on their powers — the Federal Government" of Rome. "All orders of capital punishment had to be signed by the governor" of Judea.[14] So they marched the prisoner to Pontius Pilate, "and Jesus stood before the governor."

Now Pontius Pilate undoubtedly figured prominently in Nephi's concept of world judgment, for he was a prominent figure in the trial. His importance is historical, moreover, as well as theological, since he represented to Judea the whole world empire of Rome. Like our high government officials, he was not just one man acting on his own. He had constituents who had put him in office and kept him there as long as he did not violate their public trust and confidence. Some of the Romans liked him and others did not, but for better or for worse he reflected something of every one of them in what he did, especially in his official public acts. Most politicians have deep-seated beliefs and convictions about their jobs which form their public policies and platforms; and they usually have a strong sense of civic responsibility. Some of them, like Pilate, are overly concerned with public relations; and some, I suppose, are crooks through and through. But it seems to me that most of them at least try very hard to be honorable public servants, worthy of the public that keeps them in office. On the other hand, however, sometimes that public itself is not too honorable; and then it seeks and usually gets politicians who reflect that fact quite accurately, for the public, regardless of its morals, does not want to be misrepresented. We should thus be able to learn a lot about people by taking a good look at their politics and their politicians.

Pontius Pilate has been extolled as a saint by some. In the minds of most Christians, however, there has always been something devious and questionable about him. But whatever he was, he was the official representative of government in that world which condemned the Lord and executed him by crucifixion. That has always been a strange and compelling paradox to those of us who accept him as our Savior. Think of it! Jesus had to have a formal trial in a criminal court under a secular judge and be condemned to death by the law of the land and sentenced and executed by the state! Why? we ask, just like those disciples. And the answer comes back with humiliating force: it was not for anything he did, but rather for what *we* have done, for he suffered all that to save us from our sins and from the temporal and spiritual death which they have caused. There are profound typological implications in Pilate's treatment of Christ, especially in view of Nephi's pronouncement of that trial as a world judgment. They fling a smarting accusation not only at Pilate but at his world, and at ours as well! That accusation, furthermore, stings those of us who believe in him most of all. He may save the others from temporal death, but only to be resurrected unto judgment where they will pay for their sins in full.[15] In a very real and significant sense Christ suffered all that in a special way for the believers — and *because* of them.

Isn't it an amazing thing to watch our Christian world (it used to be the pagan world!) as it attempts to restrict the significance of that trial to the long ago and the far away? They want to lock it up in the first century and keep it there forever and forever. The idea that history repeats itself and that the same attitudes and value judgments and spectacular blunders of men keep recurring in the world is especially bothersome today. We like, instead, to think in terms of human perfectibility and unlimited progress. But there it is anyway, that haunting trial. It's typical, isn't it — as Nephi suggests. It's a little model of a big world; and it doesn't make any difference whether you look first at the model and then at the world or first at the world and then at the model: the same things are there either way — the same secular attitudes toward Christ, the same spurious judgments of him, the same evasive reasoning of worldly men which is amazingly alike in every generation. As one commentator puts it: "In the case of Pilate it came to a most dramatic expression, but nevertheless we should not regard it as something exceptional. In a sense you may say that this world is like an immense courtroom, where the Son of Almighty God is on trial, and where the world is re-enacting the same drama in every period of history."[16]

Pontius Pilate typifies those secular souls who get involved in religious matters against their will. He had nothing against Judaism, as long as it kept its distance and didn't make too much noise. But he didn't like dealing with the Jews, and especially with their leaders. Not too long before, he had slain some Galileans who were sacrificing at an altar, and the leaders of the Jews had taught him a lesson he would never forget. They had raised some objections to that (and a few other things) in Jerusalem which apparently got him into quite a bit of trouble. Had they sought and obtained redress for those wrongs through the laws of Pilate's own government? It seems likely, but my best guess is that no one really knows. And now, all of a sudden, here they were again, insisting on their rights. They had a prisoner with them, too, and they were demanding that he be punished. Pilate could see trouble ahead and he didn't like it. But he didn't know exactly what to do about it either.

He told the Jews to take the prisoner and judge him according to their law. They had already done that, of course, and there was no doubt as to the verdict: it had been unanimous. He was guilty all right, they assured Pilate, but "it is not lawful for us to put any man to death." Pilate must have trembled a bit as he learned that capital charges were being brought against the prisoner: it was going to be harder than he had thought to try this case. And when he asked what the charges were, there was a pious chime of righteousness in their voices as they answered: "If he were not a habitual criminal, we would not have delivered him up unto thee" (John 18:30).[17] They remind us of the extremely corrupt and intensely respectable Laban, whose words carried that same indulging ring as he said to Laman: "Behold thou art a robber, and *I* will slay thee!" (1 Ne. 3:13; emphasis added). And Pilate knew that any law student could demonstrate beyond all question that they were well within their rights.

The first interview, furthermore, revealed that Pilate was bothered by the prisoner himself. Like many other people he was uncomfortable in the presence of Christ. Jesus made him nervous, and Pilate's superstitious temperament had prompted him to circumvent, if possible, the responsibility of trying the Lord. He claimed to be the king of those Jews, but he would answer nothing to their charges. That was an amazing thing to Pilate, and so he marveled at it. The whole thing was putting him on the spot, and his political stature was at stake. But there was one thing he simply could not afford, and that was another insurrection. He had already had too much trouble with the authorities. And so, with the greatest reluctance, he took Jesus from the mob and began his indictment of him.

But right from the beginning Pilate had been looking for a way out of his difficulty. He discovered that Herod, tetrarch of Galilee and one of the Roman Empire's "junior executives," was in Jerusalem at the time. This gave him an opportunity he couldn't afford to miss. He knew also that Jesus was accused of stirring up the people, "teaching throughout all Jewry, beginning from Galilee to this place." And so, he would refer the matter to Herod. It was as simple as that. Jesus was "technically" under his jurisdiction anyway. What a relief that must have been to Pilate! No doubt he congratulated himself as he passed Jesus on to Herod.

But Herod didn't want the responsibility of trying Jesus either, even though he thought he did at first. He had been as pleased as Pilate when he took charge of the prisoner with such gusto. He had been delighted to do it, for his curiosity was getting the best of him. He had heard a lot about this man, and he thought he would enjoy seeing him in person. He even hoped that Jesus would "entertain" him by performing some of his signs and wonders. But as Herod "questioned with him in many words," he began to experience the fears that had previously gripped Pilate. He, too, was uneasy in Jesus' presence. The ominous silence of Jesus, the uproar and confusion of the chief priests and scribes as they "stood and vehemently accused him," and his solemn and foreboding refusal to answer the charges—these things soon brought the mirth making and gaiety of Herod to a halt. He made friends with Pilate that day, for now they had something in common: an overwhelming desire to steer clear of Christ. After his one-sided conversation with Jesus he could *sympathize* with the governor's problem, but he wanted no part of solving it for him. And so he began acting as all godless men act sooner or later when they come face to face with Jesus Christ: "And Herod with his men of war set him at nought, and mocked him, and arrayed him in a gorgeous robe, and sent him again to Pilate."

When Pilate realized that he could no longer avoid the perplexity of trying Christ, he resolved anew to do as his conscience had bade him all along and set him free. In view of circumstances he knew it would be difficult at best. He was already apprehensive about the prisoner, to say nothing of the mob; and now as he sat on the judgment seat a message came from his wife that increased his anxiety. She had been distressed by a frightening dream and warned, "Have thou nothing to do with that just man: for I have suffered many things this day in a dream because of him." That didn't help matters much. It served only to aggravate his superstitious fears. But she did have a point, he thought, and he decided to follow her advice: he would have nothing to do with Jesus. That sounded like a good idea and an excellent philosophy of justice. He would find the quickest way to dispose of the prisoner and wind this case up. And the sooner the better.

For the second time now Pilate took the prisoner aside into his chambers for a private conference. He had hoped to learn something that would hasten the acquittal, but the philosophical density of the conversation disappointed him. It was all too deep and theoretical. Jesus was as bad as those Greeks who were always talking of things above the earth, up in the sky somewhere. Pilate had only asked whether or not he was king of the Jews, and Jesus had begun talking in metaphysical terms about a mystical kingdom that was not of this world. That kind of talk was all right for philosophers, but Pilate was the more practical type. And when Jesus brought up that other chestnut of philosophy, the problem of truth, he despaired of any profit in the interview. There were thousands of books on *that* topic in the libraries and precious little agreement among them. And so he sighed wearily and took Jesus back to the judgment hall; but not before he asked that cynical question, "What is truth?"

Pilate next tried to release the prisoner by taking advantage of a Passover custom. There were in the dungeon those surly fellows who belonged to that small core of extremely hardened criminals who scandalized even the rest of the criminals. They had no scruples whatever, and they broke all the laws, even the strict union rules of the syndicate! They gave crime a bad name and were a constant source of annoyance and trouble. Pilate selected

Barabbas, the worst of those congenital offenders. He then sought acquittal for Jesus by offering the mob this substitute victim, who was guilty of murder.

> That was supposed to be a political masterstroke, even though he knew it was exceedingly poor jurisprudence. But it failed; in fact, it backfired in his face, for the people and their leaders wanted to kill *Jesus*, not Barabbas. And Pilate, caught in his own trap, finally cried out in desperation: What shall I do then with Jesus which is called Christ? Ah! That was the crux of the matter, the real problem in his soul! And, since he was asking the mob for advice, he got it, quickly. They shouted back: "Crucify Him! Crucify Him!" But he didn't want to do that! He only wanted to get rid of Him, to get Him off his hands![18]

The tempo of things had picked up considerably by now, and like an amateur jazz musician Pilate was having trouble keeping up with it. He preferred the slower numbers anyway. Those fast tunes always made him run out of ideas. He needed a break, an intermission, time to settle down and think of something for the next set. So he took the prisoner back to the barracks and turned him over to the soldiers for a while.

But there was no respite for Jesus. We have already described the mimicry of the soldiers, but we must add here that as Pilate watched that pitiable sight he was, if anything, more to be pitied than Jesus. Still, he felt sorry for the prisoner as he watched him being abused. Like Alma, "his heart again began to sicken," though not for the same reason (see Alma 31:1). But he was an indomitable optimist, and that scene also suggested his next move. He thought of a way to elicit the pity of the mob by dramatizing the innocence of his prisoner, thereby hoping to convince them that he should be released. "Pilate therefore went forth again, and saith unto them, Behold, I bring him forth to you, that ye may know that I find no fault in him." There was an awkward silence as Jesus came forth "wearing the crown of thorns and the purple robe." And Pilate made the most of that one brief moment. Pointing to the prisoner he said, "Behold the man!" But the appearance of Jesus had an entirely different effect on the Jews than the one he had anticipated. It failed completely in its purpose, for there was no compassion in that mob as they looked upon the Savior. They were bound and determined to have him executed at all costs, and they would show him no pity, none whatsoever!

And Pilate was disappointed by their reaction to the prisoner. He was obviously disheartened by the repeated failure of his plans, and he was thoroughly disgusted with the Jews. Their resolute insistence that *he* crucify the man unnerved him. And when they persisted in their demands, he turned on them angrily and said, "Take *ye* him and crucify him: for I find no fault in him!" He was saying in effect, "You're not going to involve *me* in your miserable crimes! The man is innocent, and I want no part in his execution! If you want him crucified so badly, do it yourselves! But count me out of it completely!" And that only served to antagonize the Jews. They were unable to impose the death penalty under Roman law, and therefore Pilate would *have* to do it. "We have a law," they retorted, "and by our law he has to die, because he made himself the Son of God!"

For the third time now, Pilate took Jesus aside for a private interview. It was difficult to say who disturbed him more—the mob or the prisoner. He was troubled most of all, perhaps, by the Savior's claim to be the Son of God. "When Pilate therefore heard that saying," the Bible says, "he was the more afraid." And there was something else about that interview. Pilate had been out of patience when the prisoner wouldn't answer his question, and so he said, "Speakest thou not unto me? Knowest thou not that I have power to crucify thee and . . . to release thee?" But Jesus had answered, "Thou couldst have no power at all against me, except it were given thee from above: therefore he that delivered me unto thee hath the greater sin." It was that last part he didn't like: it was as though the Savior had told him, "Cheer up, old man. You're not as bad as Judas! You'll inherit a higher degree in hell than he will!"

By this time Pilate was in a quandary. He had no doubts about the prisoner's innocence and said so time and again in public. But there were other considerations. What does a politician *do* when he is caught in a conflict between the demands of his conscience and those of his constituents? Should he release the prisoner over the protests of the mob as his conscience directed? Or should he give in to their demands and condemn the prisoner even though he was innocent? The former choice was the *right* one; there was no question about that. But where would Jesus go if he were released? He would not be safe in Jerusalem, for that mob would find him somehow and kill him anyway. And even though the latter choice was definitely wrong, it *would* avoid an awful lot of trouble with the authorities, for Caesar and the Romans would be harder to manage than that mob if those subjugated Israelites rebelled again! And, of course, if that happened again it would be Pilate's fault, for he was supposed to keep the captives quietly in their chains!

He wondered halfheartedly if torturing the prisoner or punishing him severely would satisfy the Jews, but he didn't really think it would work. And sure enough, when he proposed to chastise Jesus and release him, they replied immediately, "If thou let this man go thou art not Caesar's friend: Whosoever maketh himself a king speaketh against Caesar! . . . Pilate saith unto them, Behold your king! . . . Shall I crucify your king?" And the chief priests answered, "We have no king but Caesar!" Pilate felt the snare closing tightly about him. He had tried everything he could think of to pacify that mob without sacrificing the prisoner. What more could he do? But he would not give in.

Let's see now, how many things *had* Pilate attempted? He had told the Jews to try Jesus according to their own laws. They had already done that and found him guilty of a capital crime, but they could not legally execute him. He had referred the Savior to a lower Roman court, but Herod refused the case and sent him back. He tried to follow the advice of his wife and have nothing to do with Jesus, but he was having a great deal to do with him. He had interviewed the prisoner three different times, but all he got out of it was philosophical talk or cryptic sayings or silence, and he didn't even have enough information to construct a brief for the defense. He had offered a substitute victim, but the mob rejected his offer. He had felt pity as his own soldiers mocked the Lord, but the mob didn't share his feelings. And he had proposed to chastise Jesus and release him, but the mob reminded him of Caesar and threatened to revolt. That makes nine attempts in all to free the prisoner without stirring up the Jews and, consequently, the authorities. And now at last he was at the end of his rope and couldn't think of anything else.

But wait! There was a solution, he thought. It wasn't a very good one, but then it *was* a solution and it might work out—at least for him. He must have felt a little foolish as he sent for that basin and ordered it filled with water, for he did it only after he "saw that he could prevail nothing, but that rather a tumult was made." That made his solution an admission of defeat as well as a disclaimer of responsibility. But he stumbled through the ceremony, presenting it as a kind of visual aid in the form of an object lesson. He "took water, and washed his hands before the multitude, saying, I am innocent of the blood of this just person: see ye to it."

And that was all right with the mob as long as Jesus was put to death. They were even willing to assume the blame in order to relieve Pilate of responsibility in the whole messy affair. And so they cried out, "His blood be on us, and on our children!" But there wasn't much comfort left in those words: the Roman governor had been outwitted by the mob, and he knew it. They had forced his hand, and he was selling out against his will and better judgment. The thoughts of condemning an innocent man haunted him, but so did that mob! Everything was slipping out of his control. And finally, when he could stand it no longer, he gave up in defeat and surrendered completely to their demands. In spite of all his reservations we are told that "Pilate, willing to content the people, released Barabbas unto them and delivered Jesus, when he had scourged him, to be crucified."

The story of Pontius Pilate is the story of a little boy in a big cage with his father's lion and his mother's lamb. The lion wanted to eat the lamb, but his mother insisted that he protect the lamb against the lion because it didn't deserve to be eaten. But his father didn't want the lion provoked either. He preferred it contented and quiet, and he didn't like to hear it roar. Now the boy didn't care too much for either of those animals, and ordinarily he wouldn't have interfered with them if they didn't bother him. But as it was, they were the pets of his parents, and he had to protect the lamb against the lion: he had to hold the lamb and he couldn't release it or that lion would get it and he would end up in the doghouse. And on the other hand, the lion wanted *only* that lamb, but he had been pacing restlessly back and forth for some time now, and if he didn't get it pretty soon, he would not only roar, but he would devour the boy along with the lamb! And the boy never was able to determine what the lamb wanted.

So what did the boy do? Well, inasmuch as he was a child, he thought as a child, and he hit upon a child's solution. His mother's name was "Conscience," and he didn't like to hear her cry. But he didn't like his father's whippings either. His father's name was

"Rome," and he had a terrible temper. The boy, accordingly, had to decide whether he would rather hear his mother cry or take a whipping from his father. That was necessary because the lion was getting out of hand.

Now, like most little boys he didn't like whippings. He thought he would rather hear his mother cry instead. And so he said, "Please don't blame me for what I'm going to do." And then he gave the lamb to the lion. It seemed like a good idea at first, but not long after that his mother began to cry. And she kept it up, too. In fact, she never did stop crying after that, for she knew the lamb should not have been eaten, and she was deeply offended by what her little boy had done.

And what finally happened to that little boy? Well, he grew older, but he never did grow up. He was always a little boy; he didn't ever become a man. And not being a man, he couldn't think like a man. And so he didn't realize until it was much too late that it is always better to take even a bad licking than it is to live with a whining conscience. And strangely enough his father was even displeased by what he did: the boy never could understand that, for he had tried so hard to keep the lion quiet. But he was never able to please his father after that. The Roman governor for all his maneuvering and scheming did not avert political disaster, as he was deposed by Caligula in A.D. 36. And soon after that, according to Eusebius, Pontius Pilate, "wearied with misfortunes," killed himself. You see, he wasn't really as bad as Judas after all or he wouldn't have waited so long to commit suicide: he would have done it right after the trial.[19]

Well, there we have it, the story of Pontius Pilate. It is a sad, tragic story, and there is something of it in most of us. It would have been an entirely different story if Pilate had followed that other alternative, the one he knew was right. But he was too worried about the consequences. That lion concerned him more at the moment than justice did. Still, we shouldn't condemn him too severely, for we don't find it too easy ourselves to "do what is right" and "let the consequence follow!" But if he had acquitted Jesus, you say, that mob would have devoured them both. Yes, I suppose that's true, for one righteous governor could not have stopped a powerful machine like that one among the Jews. Our governors can't do it alone today, either. But before they were consumed together, Jesus would have spoken to Pilate, perhaps as he later spoke to the thief on the cross. He might have said, "Pilate, this day shalt thou sit down with me in my kingdom which is not of this world." And what if Pilate had been fortunate enough to escape the mob? He couldn't have saved the Savior ultimately, for Jesus was born to die for the sins of the world, as Nephi said. But he *could* have fought the remainder of his days against spiritual wickedness in high places. And even if he had been condemned at Rome, the Christians would have taken him in. John would have been the first to seek him out and say, "Pilate, won't you come to our house and live with me and Mary?" And how the disciples would have loved him! And Peter, who didn't have the strength of his convictions during the trial, would have been ashamed in his presence: he would have looked upon Pontius Pilate as the supreme example of judicial righteousness, that tough-minded justice which is never cowed before the forces of evil no matter how strong or popular or respectable they become. And Paul might even have written a letter to him later on, as he did to Timothy and Philemon. And Pontius Pilate would have been taken by our own courts as their symbol of equal justice for all before the law. And we would have referred proudly to our best judges and governors as the "Pontius Pilates" of Utah and Maine and California and Washington, D.C. But that's all dreaminess, isn't it? That's not how it is today. Pontius Pilate's name is linked instead with corruption in the legal profession. He is the type of everything that is evil in jurisprudence. He is the outstanding example, not of righteous judgment but of *world* judgment. And he represents especially all of those judicial pawns who allow themselves to be used and manipulated in the sophisticated game of modern legalized crime. Pontius Pilate stands today in a place reserved specifically and solely for him as the supreme example and archetype of the judicial murderer! And let us remember that Pilate never did forget the last words Jesus spoke to him: "He that delivered me unto thee hath the greater sin." Yes, the sin of Judas was greater than the sin of Pilate. But how much greater? Pilate must have asked that question over and over again for years, until it finally drove him to suicide!

Now, if we look closely at the trial of Jesus, viewing it through the eyes of Nephi, we see all the elements of world judgment. There they are in miniature. The principals in that trial had the same mental attitudes toward the Savior that we see today on every hand. Many of our people sound just like the attorney for the defense in the modern counterpart of that trial. They find no fault in Jesus and they see great value in what he represents. They come to his church, listen to the words of eternal life, marvel at the wisdom of the scriptures, and generally benefit by his teachings. But they don't want to be considered too "religious" by men of the world. And so they just accept all of the by-products of the gospel without accepting the gospel. The whole business of redemption is superfluous in their judgment. When we preach "Christ and him crucified" today, it is just as much a stumbling block to them as it was to the Jews, and they think it every bit as foolish as the Greeks thought it was. The thing that really matters is that the church is a "going concern": they can't stand inefficiency, and so the church for them must be a smashing success, as though it were a thriving business or something. But when you ask them what they believe — well, they want to be "open-minded" and "objective." They haven't made up their minds about that yet, and they won't until all the "facts" are in. They are perfectly willing, of course, to *consider* any point of view, for that's an indication of maturity according to them; but they won't commit themselves to one, no matter what it is. They will, however, argue either side of any question at the drop of a hat without having any convictions about it one way or the other!

Well now, isn't that an amazing turn of events! There was a time when it really meant something to be a Christian. People used to believe that they had to forsake the world in order to follow Christ and vice versa. Those who were of the church were not of the world, even though they were in it. It was impossible to belong to the world and the church at the same time. But today, the pagan world and the Christian church have embraced each other with open arms. It is not only possible but *fashionable* to belong to both. Men of the world are in the church; and they are quite comfortable in it. They don't see much difference, apparently, between the world and the church; and that, I fear, is not entirely their fault! But don't let them fool you. They are not really *of* the church at all, even though they are in it. It's just an organization to them, like other organizations. It is certainly *not* the kingdom of God! That notion is a "theological hangover," the medieval ecclesiology of less enlightened and more gullible souls. And what do these people think about the Savior? Well, he was a wonderful teacher, of course, and a great man—even a *perfect* man—but a man, nevertheless. He did not come to redeem them from their sins, but to teach them how to live. And his death was not expiatory in any degree. It was a tragic thing, of course, for he was maltreated and *grossly* misunderstood. But the real value of his example is that he inspires them to *live* their religion. And they want to be like him, for he had enough moral courage to *practice* what he preached. And when he died, he was dying for his *principles*, not for the sins of the world!

Two thousand years ago the Roman governor had those same extremely pragmatic notions about everything, and so did his world. The prevailing secular philosophy which found expression in his desire to have nothing to do with Jesus was widespread and commonplace, especially in religious matters. And it showed up, not only among the practical, hardheaded Romans, but in Israel, too. Have you ever really stopped to notice the people who came into direct contact with the Savior? They form three distinct and identifiable groups. Two of those groups were small minority elements in the fractious society of Pilate's world. The first group comprised that handful of avowed and zealous enemies of Christ. They were the conspirators headed by Caiaphas and other leaders of the Jews; and like dedicated unbelievers today, they campaigned relentlessly against Christianity, for they were filled with deep, embittered hatred of Jesus Christ and everything he represented.

There was a second group of zealous and dedicated believers in the Holy Land. They comprised that small nucleus of the Savior's loyal and devoted followers. They were a sorry lot in some ways, for they were full of weaknesses: even Peter, their leader and chief Apostle, denied his Lord with curses, and three different times at that; and all of them had forsaken him in the garden and fled for their lives when the chips were down. But they were humbled by their weaknesses, and they became men of strength whose influence carried far beyond Judea and Galilee, for Jesus made them his witnesses and sent them out among the nations to bring his spiritual kingdom into their secular world.

But the third group was a big one, that vast and variegated sea of humanity represented by Pontius Pilate—the masses of people who came into contact with Jesus Christ. There were thousands of them, and they were thoroughly fascinated with

Jesus. They were the common people who "heard him gladly." A few of them did become his followers later on, but if they changed their loyalties at all, they usually went over to that other group and joined Caiaphas. Jesus never ceased to amaze them with his miracles; and like their spiritual father, Pilate, they never ceased to marvel at him. Listen to these graphic descriptions of that huge third group:

> And a great multitude from Galilee followed him, and from Judea, and from Jerusalem, and from Idumea, and from beyond Jordan; and they about Tyre and Sidon, a great multitude (Mark 3:7–8).

> And his fame went throughout all Syria. . . . And there followed him great multitudes of people from . . . Decapolis (Matt. 4:24–25).

> And the multitude cometh together again, so that they could not so much as eat bread. And when his friends heard of it, they went out to lay hold on him: for they said, He is beside himself (Mark 3:20–21).

> And he spake to his disciples that a small ship should wait on him because of the multitude, lest they should throng him (Mark 3:9).

Now that sounds like his ministry was very successful, doesn't it? Yes, indeed. But those same descriptions also tell us *why* those crowds flocked to him from every quarter. They came to him in droves

> when they had heard what great things he did. . . . For he had healed many; insomuch that they pressed upon him for to touch him, as many as had plagues (Mark 3:8, 10).

> And he came down . . . and stood . . . [with] a great multitude of people . . . which came to hear him, and to be healed of their diseases . . . and they were healed. And the whole multitude sought to touch him: for there went virtue out of him, and healed them all (Luke 6:17–19).

> And his fame went throughout all Syria: and they brought unto him all sick people that were taken with divers diseases and torments, and those which were possessed with devils, and those which were lunatick, and those that had the palsy; and he healed them (Matt. 4:24).

> And great multitudes came unto him, having with them those that were lame, blind, dumb, maimed, and many others, and cast them down at Jesus feet; and he healed them: Insomuch that the multitude wondered, when they saw the dumb to speak, the maimed to be whole, the lame to walk, and the blind to see (Matt. 15:30–31).

Yes, Jesus was an amazing healer and an interesting preacher, too. And he had lots of followers — thousands of them!

You could go through the streets and marketplaces of any city where he had been and feel the enthusiasm of the crowds. He was clearly the central topic in their buzzing conversations, and the excited hum of talk went on and on. But then one day something happened to change all that. Jesus spoke to that huge audience about their *reasons* for following him; and after that they weren't so willing to go tagging along behind him anymore. They still talked about him in the cities, but the excitement of their conversations had subsided somewhat. They were calmer now; and sometimes they would even whisper when they spoke of him. This is how it happened:

The Twelve who had been sent out by Jesus returned one day, and he went with them to a mountain on the northern shore of the Sea of Galilee. They wanted to tell him "all things, both what they had done, and what they had taught" (Mark 6:30). But true to form the crowd learned of it somehow.

> And a great multitude followed him, because they saw his miracles which he did on them that were diseased (John 6:2).

> And the people . . . ran afoot thither out of all cities, . . . and came together unto him. And Jesus . . . was moved with compassion toward them, because they were as sheep not having a shepherd (Mark 6:33–34).

> And he received them, and spake unto them of the kingdom of God, and healed them that had need of healing (Luke 9:11).

And when evening came he fed that big crowd, over five thousand of them in all, with a few small loaves and fishes. "They sat down in ranks, by hundreds and by fifties. . . . And they did all eat and were filled." And as usual, they marveled at him for that. "Those men, when they had seen the miracle that Jesus did, said, This is of a truth that prophet that should come into the world" (Mark 6:40, 42; John 6:14). And when the meal was over that crowd thought so much of him for feeding them miraculously that they wanted to "take him by force, to make him a king" (John 6:15). But Jesus eluded them somehow, and they bedded down for the night. He then sent his disciples across the Sea of Galilee in a boat and went up alone into the mountain to pray. And later that night Jesus left the crowd sleeping on the shore and walked across the Sea of Galilee to join his disciples in the boat.

The next morning there was a stir on both shores of the Sea of Galilee. At Gennesaret, where Jesus landed, he received the usual welcome from another crowd, just like the one on the northern shore.

> And when the men of that place had knowledge of him, they sent out into all the country round about, and brought unto him all that were diseased (Matt. 14:35).

> And [they] ran through that whole region round about, and began to carry about in beds those that were sick, where they heard he was. And whithersoever he entered, into villages, or cities, or country, they laid the sick in the streets, and besought him that they might touch if it were but the border of his garment: and as many as touched him were made whole" (Mark 6:55–56).

Meanwhile, back at the northern shore, the crowd had discovered the absence of Jesus. That was distressing to them because he was their hero and they wanted to follow him wherever he went. And so some of them rustled up some boats and set out on the sea, while others walked around the shore toward Capernaum; and according to the story as John tells it, they were "seeking for Jesus" (John 6:24).

Well, they found him all right, but they were shocked by what he had to say to them. "Ye seek me," he said, "not because ye saw the miracles, but because ye did eat of the loaves, and were filled" (John 6:26). Now that really means something like this: "You did not seek me this time, as you usually do, so you could applaud as I do miracles; but you are here instead because you think I am a butler who will serve you bread if you follow me about." The crowd was taken aback by that; but Jesus continued: "Labour not for the meat which perisheth, but for that meat which endureth unto everlasting life, which the Son of man shall give unto you" (John 6:27). The spokesmen for that crowd had to think those words over for a moment; but then, since he was talking about labor, they asked him: "What shall we do, that we might work the works of God?" (John 6:28). And that, translated into plain language, means, "Come now, good fellow, don't speak in mystical terms. Tell us your meaning. What is this 'labor for bread' of which you speak?" And then Jesus did a funny thing. He asked that crowd for its personal loyalty: he asked them to believe on him. He said, "This is the work of God, that ye believe on him whom he hath sent" (John 6:29). And once more, that really means, "My followers are not men who follow me around out of curiosity or selfishness: they are men who *believe* in me!"

Well, imagine that! A look of consternation came over that crowd, and they seemed to be thinking: "Now this fellow has a *real* lot of gall! Why, we have made him the most successful messianic claimant to come through these parts in a long time! But he isn't satisfied with that: he wants us to believe in his divinity! This 'carpenter's son' actually expects us to believe that he is the Messiah, the Son of God!" The crowd was quiet now, and it had already begun to get smaller. You see, that crowd wanted to follow the Lord without believing in him; but Jesus wouldn't have it that way. And now the spiritual kinship between that crowd and Pontius Pilate begins to become apparent. They weren't really against Jesus, and they certainly wouldn't have condemned him; but they weren't really for him either. And they never would have faced the basic question of believing or disbelieving in him if he had not confronted them with it. They would have continued right on the rest of their lives as a kind of spiritual fan club. They would have listened to him preach, and they would have said "Amen!" whenever he mentioned something they could agree with. They would have followed him about clapping and cheering his every noble act; and they would have kept right on thanking him graciously whenever he did them a favor, like healing their sick or giving them bread. But he wanted them to make up their minds about him. Did they believe in him or not? He wanted them to quit hiding in that huge massive crowd represented by Pontius Pilate and join one of those two smaller groups. He wanted them to come right out and identify themselves, either with Caiaphas and the Sanhedrin or with Peter, James and John. But they didn't want to do that: they wanted to stay where they were, with Pontius Pilate. When it came to a personal commitment of loyalty to Jesus, they would neither give it nor withhold it; and when they finally had to face the crisis of making up their minds whether or not they accepted *Christ* along with his teachings and his way of life, they would have nothing to do with him. And like Pontius Pilate, they worked hard at that philosophy, for like him, they really believed that it would work!

And Jesus wasn't finished yet. He went on talking about the manna from heaven. He said that the manna was not the real bread of life at all, and that it was only a type of *himself!* Jesus actually told that crowd that *he* was the real bread of life!

My father giveth you the true bread from heaven. For the bread of God is he which cometh down from heaven, and giveth life unto the world. . . . I am the bread of life: he that cometh to me shall never hunger; and he that believeth on me shall never thirst. . . . Every one which seeth the Son, and believeth on him, may have everlasting life: and I will raise him up at the last day. . . . He that believeth on me hath everlasting life. I am that bread of life. . . . This is the bread which . . . a man may eat . . . and not die. I am the living bread which came down from heaven: if any man eat of this bread, he shall live for ever: and the bread that I will give is my flesh, which I will give for the life of the world. . . . Verily, verily, I say unto you, Except ye eat the flesh of the Son of man, and drink his blood, ye have no life in you. Whoso eateth my flesh, and drinketh my blood, hath eternal life; and I will raise him up at the last day. For my flesh is meat indeed, and my blood is drink indeed. . . . This is that bread which came down from heaven: . . . he that eateth of this bread shall live for ever (John 6:32–58).

Now Pontius Pilate's crowd of spiritual relatives were offended by that. They "murmured at him because he said, I am the bread which came down from heaven" (John 6:41). They had not murmured when he did miracles or gave them bread to eat, but now they grumbled, "This is an hard saying; who can hear it?" (John 6:60). And they took offense at it. "From that time many of his disciples went back, and walked no more with him" (John 6:66). There they go, the crowd of Pontius Pilate, slinking off one by one until every one of them is gone: not one of them is left. And Jesus stands there watching them go. His heart is sad, but he is not alone. There are twelve others with him. Only one of them should have sneaked off with Pilate's crowd: the rest are loyal to him, and they follow him *because* they believe in him. So when he turned to them and asked, "Will ye also go away?" they answered, "Lord, to whom shall we go? thou hast the words of eternal life. And we believe and are sure that thou art that Christ, the Son of the living God" (John 6:67–69).

The Lord would have all men understand that they do not become his followers by following him from place to place, applauding his miracles, accepting his bounteous gifts, and talking about his teachings. But that is a favorite trick of Pilate's vast worldly group in every age: they will try to do that every time! No wonder Elder Talmage was moved to write this commentary on the flesh and blood of Christ:

To eat the flesh and drink the blood of Christ was and is to believe in and accept Him as the literal Son of God and Savior of the world, and to obey His commandments. By these means *only* may the spirit of God become an abiding part of man's individual being. . . .

It is not sufficing to accept the precepts of Christ as we may adopt the doctrines of scientists, philosophers, and savants, however great the wisdom of these sages may be; for such acceptance is by mental assent or deliberate exercise of will, and has relation to the doctrine only as independent of the author. The teachings of Jesus Christ endure because of their intrinsic worth; and many men respect his aphorisms, proverbs, and His profoundly philosophical precepts, who yet reject Him as the Son of God, the Only Begotten in the flesh, the God-Man in whom were united the attributes of Deity with those of humanity, the chosen and foreordained Redeemer of mankind, through whom *alone* may salvation be attained. But the figure used by Jesus — that of eating His flesh and drinking His blood as typical of *unqualified and absolute acceptance of Himself as the Savior of men,* is of superlative import; for thereby are affirmed the divinity of His Person, and the fact of His pre-existent and eternal Godship.[20]

Now there aren't very many people in America today who really know what "unqualified and absolute acceptance" of Christ is all about. But there are *plenty* of them around who understand perfectly well the philosophy of Pontius Pilate. He wasn't the only one, you know, who washed his hands of Jesus. That whole big crowd of his did the same thing in one way or another. And they are doing it today. Where do you go anyway to get away from Pontius Pilate and his crowd? I've found that big unwieldy blob of jellyfish neutrality everywhere I've ever been. Look at them! They're not publicans and lepers and Pharisees and Roman soldiers! They're Americans! And they're alive today! They want to be broad-minded and relative and neutral about everything, and no matter what you do you can't pin them down to take a stand on anything! Not even the eels are as slippery as they are. And they feel no need of religion, except that they want the Christian church around somewhere to exert a refining influence on society. Even the Mormon Church will do, for Americans aren't as narrow-minded as they used to be. And it is really something to hear that pious cant about religious freedom in this country: it sounds like it came from a massed choir about the size of those multitudes that followed the Savior about the countrysides. Americans don't stand in the way of religious freedom. They are neutral about most things, including religion, but religious freedom is one of the few things they are definitely *for!* We are constantly reminded that our whole Western heritage is based upon it. But I'm afraid we talk so much about freedom of religion these days that we don't know what it is anymore. We seem to think it means freedom to be neutral and secular about everything. I ask you, are Americans today really interested in the freedom to believe in Christ without restraint, or do they want the freedom to reject him the same way, so that there will be nothing to restrain them from furthering their own interests? I may not be overly optimistic, but it seems to me that for the great majority of Americans (and even for some "Saints") it is the latter!

How much closer can we get, really, to the world of Pontius Pilate? People today don't reject Christ; they know better than that. But then, they don't accept him either. They just stay completely out of his way if they can, for they want nothing to do with him. And they do it en masse, the organization way, as well as individually. We are secular in today's America. Today is the era of the colossal dodge when our whole society gingerly sidesteps any direct contact with the Savior. If there is any relationship at all between Jesus Christ and the sciences, social sciences, and humanities, it is a very vague and hazy one indeed. The scriptures are pretty good books on theology, although somewhat out-of-date for us, perhaps. But they had better stay out of the sciences — especially the life sciences and geology — where they are liable to be proved wrong on a number of points. Some of our scientists give us the impression that they could tell God a thing or two about this universe! And, oh my! Aren't we flattered in America when one of those scientists says publicly on occasion that he still believes in God in this age of cybernetics and missiles and the cyclotron and mushroom clouds and outer space! And essentially the same thing can be said of the humanities and social sciences, those other pillars in our academic trinity. Mathematics and psychology, chemistry and business, music and history, sociology and art, industry and agriculture, politics and engineering, geography and education, economics and botany, animal husbandry and air science, recreation and accounting, literature and architecture — these things have no definite relationship to Jesus Christ that can be defined as either "for" or "against" him. They are neutral and secular, of course! We insist on keeping them that way, too. And why don't we just declassify religion from the humanities and reenter it under the social sciences where we seem to think it belongs? Religion in America often walks off with all the first prizes when it comes to secularism. May I ask just one question on behalf of those in our Western culture who *do* accept Christ unqualifiedly and absolutely? How do we keep from choking as we inhale the suffocating air of righteousness that hangs like an irritating smog over all this secularity? We could use some gigantic exhaust fans in this country — and especially in our religious institutions!

Pontius Pilate's legacy to America has been described in strong terms by a preacher who is obviously a scandal to modern liberal Protestantism:

> [Pilate] would have enjoyed great popularity today. Christ is tolerated among us. Christianity is given its little corner somewhere to work out its ideas and practice its ritual unmolested and in seclusion. But it does not permeate the culture of our day, much less does it occupy a place of commanding influence. It is expected to be a *follower*, not a leader of men. They talk piously about religious liberty, and they feel very magnanimous and benevolent when they preserve for Christianity a pigeonhole in the social structure. Oh no, Christ must not be persecuted, nor condemned, nor crucified. And let us be good enough to exempt His church from taxation. And let it enjoy certain concessions and privileges! And let's inscribe our coins with a pious motto, and open our legislature with prayer, and put our hands on a Bible when we take oath of office! Let's not be antagonistic to Christianity, but friendly, and tolerant—and even protective! We don't want to be like the Russians, do we?
>
> That's what gets me, this patronizing indulgence on the part of insufferably smug and independent men and women, who are religiously neutral, who themselves have no need of Christ, who really want nothing to do with him! Sometimes I think it would be much easier to bear the outright persecution of those who hate Christianity, than to suffer this complacent and sophisticated toleration of a secular world. You can't come to grips with these people. They seem to have a hard shell of indifference about them, and you can't break through it.[21]

Howard Pierce Davis pointed to that same loss of faith and lack of convictions in "modern" religion when he said that the liberal Protestants with whom he associates would not be caught dead believing in anything.[22] They have freed themselves, not from sin but from the Savior! And the gloomy thing about it is that those same Protestant liberals have mesmerized many Latter-day Saint intellectuals: in forsaking the standard works they, too, have acquired that same hard shell of secular indifference; and they also belong to that huge contemporary crowd of Pontius Pilate's spiritual descendants.

The *ubiquity* of that spineless conglomerate, moreover, is simply amazing. What's the matter with this generation? Do we seriously believe that this impotent ideology is *Christian* and that we want to share it with men like Pontius Pilate? Well, we must believe it, for we see his philosophy everywhere. It is found uptown and downtown and across town and in the semirural and rustic areas. It is espoused by the urbane, the half-cultured, and the uncouth of all ages. We see these people in the streets and on the farms. They live in apartments, motels, rented flats, dormitories, mortgaged homes, and trailer houses. They turn up in our bus depots, air terminals, railway stations, and hotel lobbies. We hear them on the radio, read about them in newspapers and magazines, and see them in the movies and on television. They are among the faculties and student bodies of trade schools, high schools, and universities. And for relaxation they go to country clubs, bars, libraries, and night clubs, yes, and even to the churches! They are not too impressed with Jesus Christ, the Son of the Living God!

> When Jesus came to Golgotha, they hanged him on a tree.
> They drove great nails through hands and feet,
> They made – a calvary!
> They crowned him with a crown of thorns,
> Red were his wounds, and deep;
> For those were crude and cruel days,
> And human flesh was cheap.
>
> When Jesus came to my hometown, they simply passed him by.
> They never hurt a hair of him;
> They only let him die.
> For men had grown more tender;
> *They* would not give him pain.
> And so they passed on down the street,
> And left him in the rain.[23]

And one more thing. We should realize that those who espouse this philosophy are apparently naive enough to think it will actually work. They don't seem to realize that Christ condemned it severely as a way of thinking. He told the neutral church at Laodicea, for example, "I know thy works, that thou art neither cold nor hot: I would thou wert cold or hot. So then because thou art lukewarm, and neither cold nor hot, I will *spue* thee out of my mouth" (Rev. 3:15–16; emphasis added). Jesus is saying that people like this make him sick. They *nauseate* him. That word "spue," you know, does not mean "spit"; it means "vomit," "regurgitate," "throw up!"[24] And those same people forget another saying which is recorded five different times in the scriptures where the Lord has said in substance, "He that is not for me is against me" (see Matt. 12:30; Mark 9:40; Luke 9:50, 11:23; 2 Ne. 10:16). That, in effect, is what he told the big crowd in the public square. It means that there are not three alternatives at all. There are only two. There are not really two little groups and one big one. It only looks that way, for the third group is strictly an illusion. In actuality there are only two groups, a big one and a little one.

Now, if you doubt that, come with me back to Galilee to the place where Jesus preached about the bread of life. The sermon is over, he is still standing there, and that small group of disciples is with him. But where is that huge third group? Well, they didn't just evaporate into the atmosphere. They went home, I suppose. But before the Lord bowed his head on the cross and "gave up the ghost," that big crowd showed up again, at least three different times.

When Jesus rode into Jerusalem on a colt, the foal of an ass, that multitude was there again to greet him. This is how the New Testament describes the way they did it: "And a very great multitude spread their garments in the way; others cut down branches from the trees, and strawed them in the way" (Matt. 21:8). "And when he was come nigh, even now at the descent of the mount of Olives, the whole multitude of the disciples began to rejoice and praise God with a loud voice for all the mighty works that they had seen" (Luke 19:37). "And the multitudes that went before, and that followed, cried, saying, Hosanna to the Son of David" (Matt. 21:9). "Blessed be the kingdom of our father David, that cometh in the name of the Lord" (Mark 11:10). "Blessed is he that cometh in the name of the Lord; Hosanna in the highest" (Matt. 21:9).

That was on Sunday. But five days later, on Friday, that same multitude showed up again, this time for the trial. They are still talking about Jesus, but their voices are louder than ever before. And what are they saying? "Crucify him! Crucify him!" And where are they standing? Well, they have gone over to that other smaller group. And who is their leader now, that man standing in front of them? It's not Pilate, for he is on the judgment seat. It's Caiaphas! You see, his little group has become a huge, massive group, and the third group has disappeared altogether!

And it's no accident that this is a public trial, either. It *had* to be, as Hugh Nibley would say, "in the absence of television!"[25]

Caiaphas and the conspirators could not have created a mob out of nothing: they had to have a big neutral crowd to work with first. They were expert mass psychologists who knew all about the so-called modern game of molding public opinion and changing and manipulating it to serve their ends. Human relations and advertising, moreover, were their special fields. Pontius Pilate's big third group was no match for them. In the hands of Caiaphas and the conspirators, that huge neutral crowd easily became the mob at the trial shouting "Crucify him! Crucify him!" And they meant it, too, for at heart they really belonged in that first group with Caiaphas all along! That's why they were offended by that sermon on the bread of life, and why, incidentally, Elder Talmage has referred to Jesus Christ as "the greatest offender in history"![26]

And that same multitude also came to the crucifixion, this time in their true characters as disciples of Caiaphas. They are still talking about Jesus. Once more, let's read the story in the New Testament.

> And the people stood beholding. And the rulers also with them derided him, saying, . . . let him save himself if he be Christ, the chosen of God. And the soldiers also mocked him, . . . saying, If thou be the King of the Jews, save thyself (Luke 23:35-37).

> And they that passed by reviled him, wagging their heads, and saying, Thou that destroyest the temple, and buildest it in three days, save thyself. If thou be the Son of God, come down from the cross. Likewise also the chief priests mocking him, with the scribes and elders, said, He saved others; himself he cannot save. If he be the King of Israel, let him now come down from the cross, and we will believe him. He trusted in God; let him deliver him now, if he will have him: for he said, I am the Son of God (Matt. 27:39-43).

> And one of the malefactors which were hanged railed on him, saying, If thou be Christ, save thyself and us (Luke 23:39).

> Now when the centurion, and they that were with him, watching Jesus, saw the earthquake, and those things that were done, they feared greatly, saying, Truly this was the Son of God (Matt. 27:54).

> Certainly this was a righteous man. And all the people that came together to that sight, beholding the things which were done, smote their breasts and returned (Luke 23:47-48).

If we in America today could only learn a lesson from Pontius Pilate, instead of devouring his philosophy as though it were ambrosia! There are those who say that we learn from history only what we don't learn from history. I sincerely hope they are wrong.

But I know this: we should be able to see in Pilate's tragic end the ultimate end of his philosophy carried to its logical conclusion. And we had better learn from it, for it tends surely and inevitably to suicide. The neutral secularism of America, and especially of her religious institutions, is a dangerous element in our current national panic and pessimism and manic depression. And it could lead eventually to national suicide, too — make no mistake about that! But it won't if enough Americans get out of that big crowd soon enough and go over to that little group with Peter, James, and John and a few other Americans who worship the God of the land, who is Jesus Christ. But we are in serious trouble if we wait until that crowd becomes a mob, for then it is too late! There is not much difference, remember, between the crowd of Pontius Pilate and the mob of Caiaphas. Both of those men bear a strong resemblance to Judas. And you know, all three of them took their own lives, really, for although Caiaphas didn't literally kill himself, he did commit spiritual suicide by what he did. And so did the conspirators. And so will we — unless we get out of their company before it is too late!

I don't suppose it would be sporting to remind Americans that here in this country it was not unbelievers who banded together in Missouri and Illinois and swooped down upon the Latter-day Saints like marauding hordes of desert Bedouin to send them flying in all directions. And even if the Mormons had been what they were accused of being — that "insidious blight and festering sore" of America — how could anyone justify Missouri's Governor Boggs in issuing an official "Order of Extermination" against them and unleashing the vicious state militia to perpetrate, say, the Haun's Mill Massacre at Shoal Creek? I suppose it was all right because it was *religious,* or because it was done in the name of civic virtue by citizens of the United States whose patriotic instincts had been abrased and who were only "protecting their rights"! But history, I'm afraid, will refer to *that* and not the Mormons as:

> A blot that will remain a blot, in spite
> Of all that grave apologists can write;
> And though a Bishop try to cleanse the stain,
> He'll rub and scour the crimson spot in vain.[27]

And many of the Latter-day Saints would be offended if I were to tell them that I was almost twenty-five years of age before I heard the basic doctrines of the Book of Mormon, the Fall of man and the Atonement of Jesus Christ, although I was born and raised in the Church and *active* all my life. Now that is partly my fault, I know; but I can't take all the blame, as I did manage to win a couple of those 100-percent awards for perfect attendance. And, since I have been converted to Jesus Christ by the Book of Mormon, I speak of him occasionally. I didn't do that before I was converted because there were too many other interesting things to talk about—like the parables, the welfare plan, the Sermon on the Mount, the good life, the gold and green ball, the MIA basketball tournament, the Golden Rule, the internal consistency of the Book of Mormon, the Word of Wisdom, the golden plates, the ruins of South America, the Three Nephites, the great and abominable church, the Hill Cumorah pageant, eternal marriage, and the blood stain on the floor of Carthage Jail, to mention only a few. But my interests have changed somewhat since then. Oh, I still believe in those things and talk about them once in a while, but not in the same way as before. And I usually talk about other things whenever I'm called to speak in sacrament meetings or to teach Sunday School classes. I talk about all of the interesting things I found *inside* the Book of Mormon when I finally stopped worshiping that book and started reading it. I talk most of all about the Atonement of Jesus Christ and the Fall of man which made it necessary. I spend less time "proving" the Book of Mormon and more time teaching its doctrines and persuading the Latter-day Saints to believe in Christ and repent of their sins. I tell them that "the natural man is an enemy to God" (Mosiah 3:19), that all men are "carnal, sensual, and devilish by nature" (Alma 42:10), and that "all mankind, yea, men and women, all nations, kindreds, tongues and people, must be born again; yea, born of God, changed from their carnal and fallen state, to a state of righteousness, being redeemed of God, becoming his sons and daughters" (Mosiah 27:25). For only in this way can "they become new creatures; and unless they do this, they can in nowise inherit the kingdom of God" (Mosiah 27:26). I speak of other things, too, but they are all related to the Fall and the Atonement—the birth of the spirit, the suffering in Gethsemane, the Crucifixion, the blood of Christ, the forgiveness of sins, justice and mercy, the grace of God, repentance and the change of heart which comes from it, and the peace of conscience that came to converts in the Book of Mormon when "a mighty change was also wrought in their hearts, and they humbled themselves and put their trust in the true and living God" (Alma 5:13), who is Jesus Christ.

Now, I've discovered that most people in our sacrament meetings appreciate that kind of talk once in a while. But every now and then I speak in a ward which has that stiff, secular spirit of Pontius Pilate about it. And the people there are astonished by that kind of preaching at first, and then bored by it: after the initial shock is over, it's a ho-hum affair until I get through and someone else goes on with those other topics, the ones they are more used to. And I can tell by the looks on their faces that they are thinking, "Who is this Protestant? And where did he get all of those medieval concepts?" But they are somewhat puzzled, too, for those concepts came straight from the Book of Mormon, not from some old sectarian catechism. And some of them have been quite frankly indignant about it, and have said to me, "Must we listen to this antiquated theology? That kind of talk may be all right for monks and ministers, and for a few extremely emotional and misguided Latter-day Saints, but it's taboo in *this* ward." And I usually say, "Yes, I can see that." Then both they and I are happier when we go our separate ways — and those ways *are* separated, believe me.

And so the typological concept of world judgment speaks to every age, our own included. Those four words, "judged of the world," are *alive* with meaning, for by them Nephi indicts those who merely ignore the Savior as well as those who reject and condemn him openly and bitterly. And every time we read the vision of Nephi we see those incriminating words: "And I looked and beheld the Lamb of God, that he was taken by the people; yea, the Son of the everlasting God was judged of the world; and I saw and bear record." And those words remind us every time of Pontius Pilate first of all, and then of Caiaphas and Judas.

In that great and last day when all shall stand before this man whom the world because of their iniquity have judged to be a thing of naught, the tables will be turned and *he* will be the judge. And in that day he will separate the sheep from the goats, the wheat from the tares, the righteous from the wicked, the children of heaven from the children of hell.[28] It is not entirely correct to say, as some do, that Pontius Pilate handed down the most important decision of all time, for Jesus Christ will eventually decide the guilt or innocence of all men everywhere. He came into the world for judgment: that was the purpose of his life, for according to his own words, his Father sent him to "be lifted up upon the cross"; and as he had been lifted up by men, "even so should men be lifted up by the Father" to stand before him at the last day (see 3 Ne. 27:13-22; see also D&C 19:4, 15-24; 45:2-6; et al.). In fact, when we really stop to think about it, if we ever do, the Father actually intended that he be "judged of the world," so that the world in turn might be judged of him.

And there is nothing we can do to avoid that judgment—in either of its aspects. It is an awful thing to contemplate, but we, too, must try him and bring in a verdict: one way or another we *must* have an opinion of him, since we cannot remain neutral forever. That is a terrible responsibility, of course, but we cannot escape it by adopting the philosophy of Pontius Pilate. We may have all kinds of reasons for thinking that way now. But we won't bother to repeat them then, for when we finally stand before him in judgment we will realize that in the last analysis indecision or neutrality are the same things as rejection or condemnation. Who knows? God may even consider them much worse!

The Lord himself asked the Pharisees of his day, "What think ye of Christ?" A cartoon appeared some years ago on the editorial page of the *Deseret News* that asked the same question of our generation. There in the foreground was Pontius Pilate, chin in hand, with a puzzled searching look on his face as though he were involved in deep thought. In the background were the soldiers and the restless milling mob. And there between them stood Jesus, hands bound, dressed in Herod's robe. The words of that cartoon said, "Like Pilate, a question we all must answer—What to do with Jesus?"

Well, what will *you* do with Jesus? That's an individual problem, you know, and it's coming right at you. Like all of us, you need the revealed wisdom of God—not the humanly gener- ated wisdom of man—in order to answer that question properly, for you cannot dodge it, and you cannot pass it on to someone else. But remember this as you wrestle with that awful question: when you have finally answered it correctly, you will have dis- covered the pearl of greatest price: you will have found your Lord and Savior—the King of Kings—with the crown of thorns!

# Bibliography

*Monographs on the Trial*

Josef Blinzler, *The Trial of Jesus: The Jewish and Roman Proceedings Against Jesus Christ Described and Assessed from the Oldest Accounts* (Westminster: Newman Press, 1959). Also available in German as *Der Prozess Jesu* (Regensburg: F. Pustet, 1955). One of the best accounts of the trials.

Gert Buckheit, *Judas Iskarioth: Legende, Geschichte, Deuting* (Gutersloh: Rufer-Verlag, 1954).

Walter Marion Chandler, *The Trial of Jesus From a Lawyer's Standpoint*, 2 vols. (Atlanta: Harrison, 1956). One volume deals with the Jewish trial, and the other with the Roman.

Alberto Entralgo Cancio, *Marti Ante el Proceso de Jesus* (Habana: Editorial La Verdad, 1956).

Hyman Elias Goldin, *The Case of the Nazarene Reopened* (New York: Exposition Press, 1948). A "vanity press" publication, this work treats the trial from a Jewish point of view.

George Fox Gresham, *Jesus, Pilate and Paul; an Amazingly New Interpretation of the Trial of Jesus Under Pontius Pilate, with a Study of Little Known Facts in the Life of Paul Before His Conversion* (Chicago: Isaacs, 1955). Based on the author's "The Jews, Jesus, and Christ," a Jewish point of view.

Richard Wellington Husband, *The Prosecution of Jesus; its Date, History and Legality* (Princeton: Princeton University Press, 1916). Husband is convinced that the trial of Jesus should be approached through Roman, not Hebrew, criminal law.

Alexander Taylor Innes, *The Trial of Jesus Christ, a Legal Monograph* (Edinburgh: T. and T. Clark, 1899). There is also a second edition, 1905.

John Evan Richards, *The Illegality of the Trial of Jesus* (New York: Platt & Peck, 1915). Bound with this is Aiyar S. Srinivasa, *The Legality of the Trial of Jesus*. Richards was Associate Justice of the First District Court of Appeals of California. Srinivasa was High Court Vakil and editor of the *Madras Law Journal*.

Giovanni Rosadi, *The Trial of Jesus* (New York: Dodd, Mead, 1905).

Rene Jules Rousseau, *Un Aspect Nouveau du Proces de Jesus* (Paris: A. Bonne, 1957).

George Washington Thompson, *The Trial of Jesus; a Judicial Review of the Law and Facts of the World's Most Tragic Courtroom Trial* (Indianapolis: Bobbs-Merrill, 1927). Thompson was Professor of Law at the University of Florida.

*LDS Treatments of the Trial*

Oscar Walter McConkie, *A Dialogue at Golgotha; an Analysis of Judaism and Christianity, and of the Laws, Government, and Institutions of the Jews, and the Jewish and Roman Trials of Jesus of Nazareth* (Salt Lake City: Oscar W. McConkie, 1945).

James Edward Talmage, *Jesus the Christ* (Salt Lake City: Deseret Book, 1949). The Jewish and Roman trials are both covered in chapter 34.

---

# Notes

1. Peter H. Eldersveld, *The Truth for Today* (Chicago: The Back to God Hour, 1952), 23.

2. See bibliography for a list of monographs on the trial.

3. Herbert C. Wright, *A Study of Certain Typological References to the Atonement Found in Genesis, Exodus, and Numbers* (Provo: Brigham Young University, 1955), especially chapters 1 and 3, entitled respectively, "What Is a Type?" and "Book of Mormon Typology." This thesis is unpublished but available at BYU Library.

4. It is impossible to imagine a more secular discipline than history, which is simply the best method human wisdom has been able to devise for obtaining information about the past. *Historia* is a Greek word for describing the scholarly attitude of serious critical inquiry into anything by any human being whatever. This word, which implicitly rejects revelation as a valid source of information in any human study, must often be translated as "knowledge-seeking" or "science," but not in the experimental sense of modern laboratory science. The *histor* is thus the knowledge-expert in any field, the *aner sophikos* who knows whatever he knows about this world by human wisdom; he is not the *aner mantikos*, the man of faith who knows

things that may or may not be of this world by the revealed wisdom of God. History and science are therefore different aspects of the same thing, although they have been thoroughly differentiated in modern times. They are both secular disciplines which share the common attitude of human critical inquiry with all other secular disciplines. Science deals with the formation and testing of hypotheses about the observable realities of matter and energy. The present, accordingly, constitutes its only legitimate province, since the data of yesterday (or tomorrow) cannot be observed. History must therefore *reconstruct* yesterday's data indirectly and reflectively by examining words, the verbal reports or surviving *testimonia* of witnesses from and about the past.

The seventeenth century, by exalting science above all else, came to despise history, which therefore remained crude and elementary throughout the eighteenth century. But a terrific resurgence of historical interest occurred in the nineteenth century, after the meteoric rise of scientific thought had dealt its near-fatal blows to the older reliance on metaphysics and revealed religion. The rise of modern history as a new secular religion was thus precipitated by the plummeting decline of both rational and pistic forms of transcendentalism in the West. History was at least compatible with "modern" thought; and modern thinkers have therefore relied on it to assume the traditional functions of metaphysics and revelation by answering the basic questions of human life without going even one iota beyond the pale of human wisdom.

The very different orientations of history and revealed religion, needless to say, have polarized twentieth-century studies of the life of Jesus. The Bultmannians, impatient with the naive source criticism of older humanist scholars, have invented their critical *Formgeschichte* by de-emphasizing faith in the redemptive Christ and applying to the human life of Jesus the exacting historical methods of classical scholarship, and more particularly of Homeric studies. On this scheme, of course, the modern emasculation of Christ's redemptive mission was inevitable, since (1) *classical scholarship was derived from the Greeks,* who flatly rejected anything smacking of Near Eastern supernaturalism; (2) *Bultmann was himself a classicist,* a scientifically trained neohumanist openly hostile to the supernatural gospel which gave birth to the eschatological thinking of the ancient Near East; and (3) *no Greek (or Roman) in his right mind ever had "faith" in Zeus (or Jupiter)* in anything even remotely resembling the same sense in which David had faith in Elohim or Paul had faith in Christ. The Greco-Roman civilizations, in a word, were driven by the secular knowledge-spirit of western Europe, not by the Near Eastern spirit of redeeming faith. The Barthians, conversely, who regard the redemptive functions of Christ's messianic mission as indispensable to the salvation of human beings, have provided the principal alternative to Bultmann's overly historical methods by constructing the reformed neo-orthodoxy of traditional Protestantism. They have failed, however, to explain why their "God who speaks" never says anything, or how a deity "wholly other" than themselves can be their God; but they have at least shown that the quest of the historical Jesus, which is academically respectable and very popular today, is a secular quest derived from the Greco-Roman West that can only obscure the Christ of faith, who comes to us from the ancient Near East.

5. Much of the following discussion is taken from Hugh Nibley, "The Way of the Wicked," in *An Approach to the Book of Mormon* (Salt Lake City: Deseret News Press, 1957), 315–35. Those who think syndicated crime is a product of the modern world will be enlightened by this study. I highly recommend it. Nibley is professor emeritus of ancient history and religion at BYU.

6. Nibley, *An Approach to the Book of Mormon,* 317.

7. Ibid., 315.

8. Ibid., 317.

9. Ibid., 315–16.

10. Although this passage is rendered in the KJV as if the indicative mood were intended, the imperative mood, which I have followed here, is identical in form.

11. The feeling of deep love in the traitor's kiss is inherent in the preposition κατά, which is compounded with the verb meaning "kiss." This compound form is found in both Matthew and Mark. For an excellent discussion of κατά and its antonym ἀνά see F. A. Adams, *The Greek Prepositions Studied from their Original Meanings as Designations of Space* (New York: D. Appleton, 1885), 436. When κατά is compounded with the verb meaning "eat," the resulting compound form means "devour greedily." In the same way, when κατά is compounded with "kiss," the resultant compound means "kiss passionately, with warmth and tenderness." Use by both Matthew and Mark of the aorist [undefined] tense, which states the mere occurrence of verbal activity (without defining the aspect of activity or *how* verbal action occurs), also leaves open the possibility that the kissing was done more than once. This possibility is implicit in the name of the "aorist" tense, since ἀόριστος means "undefined," "indefinite," or "indeterminate" specifically because it lacks definers or limiters known as ὅροι, "definitions," "limits," "boundaries," "frontiers," etc.

12. Nibley, *Approach to the Book of Mormon,* 322.

13. Ibid., 323.

14. Ibid., 329–30.

15. See Alma 11:40–41, where we read: "And he shall come into the world to redeem his people; and he shall take upon him the transgressions of those who believe on his name; and these are they that shall have eternal life, and

salvation cometh to none else. Therefore the wicked remain as though there had been no redemption made, except it be the loosing of the bands of death." See also Morm. 9:13–14.

16. From a sermon entitled "Christ Before a World Court," in Peter H. Eldersveld, *That Ye May Believe* (Grand Rapids: Eerdmans, 1950).

17. Κακὸν ποιῶν, usually rendered "malefactor," implies repeated evil doing, since the present participle makes this combination of words mean "one who does evil habitually," whereas the aorist participle would simply imply "one who has done evil."

18. See source cited in note 16, above.

19. William Smith, *A Dictionary of the Bible* (Philadelphia: John C. Winston, 1948), 519–20. See also Jacques Roergas de Serviez, *The Roman Empresses: or, the History of the Lives and Secret Intrigues of the Wives of the Twelve Caesars* (New York: H. S. Nichols, 1913), 1:167: this source says that Caligula "punished the misbehavior of the governors of provinces, among whom was Pontius Pilate, procurator of Judea, who, being convicted of bribery, extortion, and other crimes, was banished to Vienne, where he became his own executioner, and killed himself in despair."

20. James E. Talmage, *Jesus the Christ* (Salt Lake City: Deseret Book, 1949), 342–43; emphasis added. In note 6, p. 274, Talmage calls Christ "the greatest offender in history" because those who reject the gospel take offense at him.

21. Source cited in note 16, above.

22. Howard Pierce Davis, "Things That Matter," an address delivered to the BYU student body on October 12, 1959. This address may be located in *Speeches of the Year*, a collection of devotional and forum addresses housed in the Harold B. Lee Library at BYU.

23. Adapted with only punctuation and other minor changes, such as "drove" for "drave" and "my hometown" for "Birmingham," from a poem by G. A. Studdert-Kennedy entitled "Indifference" and published in Thomas C. and Hazel D. Clark, eds., *Christ in Poetry; an Anthology* (New York: Association Press, 1952), 168.

24. The word "spue" is translated from ἐμέω, which means "vomit."

25. Source cited in note 5, above.

26. See note 20, above.

27. This anonymous quatrain is cited without source in B. H. Roberts, *A Comprehensive History of the Church of Jesus Christ of Latter-day Saints* (Salt Lake City: Deseret News Press, 1930), 1:483, note 41.

28. As C. S. Lewis has said, the last judgment will sort all men into two groups: those who have said to God, "Thy will be done," and those to whom God will say, "*Thy* will be done." The niceties of those two groups—who goes where and why, etc.—do not concern us here.

## Message Two

# The Work of Joseph Smith

*In a simple and profound essay, Curtis clarifies two aspects of Joseph's mission and two essentials of our missions in life. This is not a formal attempt to analyze the Prophet's divine commission and to evaluate the performance of his mission. It is the distillation of a letter Brother Wright wrote in 1981 to a son in the mission field in order to clarify the main responsibilities of members and missionaries to teach the gospel and to build up the Church. Curtis says concisely in conclusion that this "is what constitutes the work of Joseph Smith. Whatever else he did may have its own importance; but by far the most important thing about him is the fact that he was assigned this double mission . . . of restoring the eternal PRINCIPLES of the gospel, which are in the Book of Mormon, and the temporal PRACTICES of the Church, which are in the Doctrine and Covenants."*

*Brother Wright shows from Church history and revelations to the Prophet about himself (humbly and frankly printed in the Doctrine and Covenants) that Joseph was commended by the Lord when he did his assigned work and called to repentance when he did otherwise.*

*The basic essence of Joseph's twofold mission was thus to reveal anew the fulness of the gospel by translating and publishing the Book of Mormon, and to establish anew the true Church as the vehicle for applying and extending essential gospel principles and ordinances until "all who will hear may hear" and live accordingly (cf. D&C 1:11).*

*Ellis T. Rasmussen*
*Dean of Religious Instruction, 1976–81*
*Brigham Young University*

The Lord requires neither science nor scholarship to do his work. The Book of Mormon could easily have been discovered by early "archaeologists" and publicized by 19th-century schoolmen. But this book, as Nephi knew anciently by the Spirit, was to "be hid from the eyes of the world" because of worldly "wickedness and abominations," for the Lord himself would bring forth its words and establish them "in the mouth of as many witnesses as seemeth him good" (2 Ne. 27:8, 12, 14). Its prototext, says Nephi, will not be given to the world but "shall be delivered unto a man," and "none other . . . shall view it, save it be a few according to the will of God" (2 Ne. 27:9, 13). The man will then "deliver the words of the book . . . unto the learned," who, "because of the glory of the world and to get gain . . . and not for the glory of God," will want only the book itself and refuse to consider its words (2 Ne. 27:9–10, 15–18). "Wherefore . . . the Lord God will deliver again the book and the words thereof to him that is not learned . . . [and] say unto him: The learned shall not read . . . [the words of the book], for they have rejected them. . . . [And] I will show unto the children of men that I am able to do mine own work. . . . I am a God of miracles; . . . *I work not among the children of men save it be* according to their faith. . . . Therefore, I will . . . do a marvelous work among this people, . . . for the wisdom of their wise and learned shall perish" (2 Ne. 27:19–21, 23, 26; emphasis added).

Joseph Smith was called as a prophet because "God had a special work for him to do."[1] Lehi quotes another Joseph, the son of Jacob, as saying: "Thus saith the Lord unto me: A choice seer will I raise up out of the fruit of thy loins. . . . [And] he shall do a work . . . of great worth unto them" (2 Ne. 3:7). The Lord also told Joseph, the son of Jacob, that "I will give unto him [Joseph Smith] a commandment that he shall do none other work, save the work which I shall command him . . . for he shall do my work" (2 Ne. 3:8). The Lord thus gave Joseph Smith a specific work to do, and commanded him to do that work and that work only. If Joseph did not always follow that commandment to the letter, it is doubtless because he was immensely curious about all aspects of the world he lived in. He therefore got out of the harness occasionally and worked on things that appealed to him rather than doing the specific work he had been commanded to do; and whenever that happened, the Lord had to jerk him back into the traces in order to remind him of the true nature of his calling and to insist that, if he wanted to do the Lord's work, he would have to forgo his lesser interests.

It is important to understand the work of Joseph Smith in terms of his prophetic functions. The work he did for the Lord is correlated with two things very intimately: the Book of Mormon, which he brought forth, translated, and published to all the world; and the Doctrine and Covenants, which also came forth through him. These two books are absolutely central to his mission. What, then, is the relationship between the Book of Mormon and the Doctrine and Covenants? And how is each related to Joseph's calling? They are, to be sure, different kinds of records. The Book of Mormon is essentially a theological document, a doctrinal account of the acceptance and rejection of the *gospel* by ancient Americans, whereas the Doctrine and Covenants is basically an ecclesiastical record, a document concerned mainly with the restored *Church* as the kingdom of God on earth. This distinction, though often overlooked, is fundamental, since the Book of Mormon and the Doctrine and Covenants are both involved directly with the specific work Joseph Smith was called and commanded by the Lord to do.

The Doctrine and Covenants, as an essentially ecclesiastical document, is oriented more directly to the Church than to the gospel. This does not mean, of course, that there is no doctrine in the Doctrine and Covenants, which often discusses crucially important theological issues. But it does mean that the Doctrine and Covenants is more about the restored Church than about anything else: it treats explicit matters related to the organizational structure and temporal functions of the kingdom of God, along with its administrative protocols, policies, procedures, and practices, and the requirements of its citizens; and as such, it is primarily concerned with things like callings and ordinations, quorum activities, the performance of temple ordinances and other rituals, bishops' storehouses, problems of dealing with the unfaithful (which are also discussed in the Book of Mormon), the keeping of historical and other records, and numerous specific items such as caring for the sick or the construction and purposes of the Nauvoo House. Because it is mainly concerned with these sorts of things, one of our best instruments for understanding the Doctrine and Covenants is Church history: if we are to grasp the message of the

Doctrine and Covenants, if we are to understand it in any depth or sophistication at all, we must correlate its discussions of specific persons, places, and events with the temporal history of the restored Church. It is thus God's concern for his kingdom on earth—for all of the temporal particulars discussed in or related to the Doctrine and Covenants—which creates a fundamental part of Joseph Smith's office and calling as a prophet: it accounts for roughly half of the reason why he was called to be a prophet, and constitutes approximately half of the work he was called to do.

The Book of Mormon, on the other hand, consistently emphasizes the doctrinal subject matters of revealed theology. It is not a historical document per se:[2] it says repeatedly itself, for example, that what we would call the systematic histories of the Nephite and Jaredite peoples were compiled, not on the small plates of Nephi (where an account of revealed realities was kept by prophets), but on those "other plates," the large plates of Nephi, where historical events were recorded by the secular authority of kings and judges (see 1 Ne. 9:2; 19:1–2, 4; 2 Ne. 4:14; 5:29; and Jacob 1:3). It is this larger set of plates—the set God has not revealed to us—that we would have to search in order to discover the scientific, economic, political, social, intellectual, cultural, and artistic histories of the Nephite and Jaredite civilizations.[3] The Book of Mormon is therefore a special kind of record, for it was translated from prophetic documents by the revealed wisdom of God, not from historical documents by the humanly originated wisdom of secular scholarship. Its subject matter, accordingly, was selected and controlled by prophets, who labored under the direct supervision of the Lord himself, in order to show us the great importance of the *ministry* (see 1 Ne. 9:3–4; 19:3) to ancient Americans who accepted the gospel, and also to show us, by their withdrawal and apostasy from the gospel, what caused their decline and destruction. The Book of Mormon is thus oriented to the gospel almost exclusively. It is not a "churchy" document. It does not dwell on programs, nor is it preoccupied with things like organizational patterns or administrative procedures: you can't tell from the Book of Mormon, to put it simply, what the Sunday School was like in Zarahemla. The Church, on the other hand, is ever present in the Book of Mormon, although it is virtually confined to the background: it is always off-stage, working diligently behind the scenes, in order to present the gospel to a troubled world. It is the gospel itself, meanwhile, that occupies center stage throughout the Book of Mormon, while the Church stands alert and attentive in the wings, where it plays a supportive role. The gospel, in other words, constitutes the paramount concern of the Book of Mormon, which always presents it as primary and basic, whereas the Church remains backstage, away from the spotlight, in a secondary and instrumental capacity. The Church plays an indispensable role all through the Book of Mormon; but it does not play the central role. Its only reason for being is to make the gospel clear, to present it properly, and to interpret it faithfully unto the children of men. The Book of Mormon therefore constitutes the other half of the office and calling of Joseph Smith. It is the most important part of the reason why he was called to be a prophet; for only if "the church is built upon my gospel," saith the Lord, "will the Father show forth his own works in it" (3 Ne. 27:10) — which is to say that, if there were no gospel, there would be no Book of Mormon; and if there were no Book of Mormon, there would be no Doctrine and Covenants, for the Church would not exist. The prophetic mission of Joseph Smith is thus aligned with the Book of Mormon, which contains the eternal principles of the everlasting gospel, and with the Doctrine and Covenants, which describes the temporal practices of the Church and kingdom of God. The restoration of these two things constitutes the only work Joseph Smith was called by the Lord to do: he was to do *only* this work.[4]

The Lord clearly wants us to ponder the work of Joseph Smith in order to understand its prophetic nature and its redemptive functions and purposes. But we should focus on its central concerns, not on peripheral matters. It should neither disturb nor fascinate us too much, perhaps, to discover that Joseph Smith himself was curious about the peripheral as well as the central concerns of the kingdom, or even to learn that he postponed the Lord's work occasionally and tried to do the work of the world. The Lord rebuked him several times, as a matter of fact, for this very thing. But the point is that we need not be unduly troubled, say, by problems arising from the speculations of BYU professors about heady matters on which LDS intellectuals may be divided or confused.[5] Many issues related to work other than the work Joseph Smith was called to do are not worth resolving: we should not worry too much about them, for they often serve only to distract us from the real issues of revealed religion.[6] We must not overlook, for example, the twenty-fourth section of the Doctrine and Covenants, where both elements of the prophets work are spelled out in the first sentence. "Thou wast called and chosen to write the Book of Mormon," the Lord tells Joseph Smith, "and to my ministry" (D&C 24:1). The dual functions of the prophets mission are explicitly revealed in this brief statement. Joseph was called, first of all, "to write the Book of Mormon" — not to become its author, of course, but to retrieve its ancient prototext from metallic epigraphs buried in a sealed stone box,[7] and to translate that prototext by the gift and power of God in order to publish it as the doctrinal standard of the restoration. And secondly, the Lord tells Joseph, "thou wast called . . . to my ministry" — to the prophetic work of restoring the kingdom of God to this planet with all of its redemptive machinery intact. Thus, Joseph Smith was called to the ministry by the Lord himself; and his work as a minister was to rebuild the ancient community of Zion in the modern world — to establish the Church on the sure foundation of the gospel, to get it running again, and to ensure that it operated properly and as smoothly as possible.

Joseph Smith was fully supported in his calling by the powers of heaven. "I have lifted thee out of thine afflictions," the Lord tells him, "and have counseled thee, that thou hast been delivered from all thine enemies, and . . . from the powers of Satan and from darkness" (D&C 24:1). But he was also rebuked for neglecting the work he was called to do. "Thou art not excusable in thy transgressions" (D&C 24:2), he is told, which means that he *did* transgress — and more than once, too. Still, as all sinners have their failings, we cannot throw stones at him for this. When Joseph does something wrong, on the other hand, it gets into the Doctrine and Covenants; and in this instance God is clearly displeased with him. "Nevertheless," the Lord instructs him, "go thy way and sin no more. Magnify thine office; and . . . go speedily unto the church . . . and they shall support thee" (D&C 24:2-3). If Joseph Smith is to magnify his office, however, he must know what it is; and so must the people of the Church, if they are to support him in it. What, then, *is* his office? It is to minister unto the Church, and to bring forth the Book of Mormon — not only to publish it, but to bring its message of redemption to the Church and thence to all the world. Members of the Church, moreover, are specifically called upon to support their prophet in this. And if they do it, the Lord says, "I will bless them both spiritually and temporally; but if they receive thee not, I will send upon them a cursing instead of a blessing" (D&C 24:3-4). The Lord then gave explicit instructions to Joseph Smith, who was to forsake his secular interests and stick to his office and calling. "Thou shalt continue in calling upon God in my name, and writing the things which shall be given thee . . . and expounding all scriptures unto the church. And it shall be given thee . . . what thou shalt speak and write, and they shall hear it, or I will send unto them a cursing instead of a blessing" (D&C 24:5-6). All of these duties, whether incumbent on the prophet or upon the Church, are consistent with the dual nature of Joseph's office and calling, which was to restore both the gospel and the Church. The Lord, who required a consuming, total commitment from Joseph Smith if he was to perform his labors properly, then gave him a specific commandment with a promise, saying: "Thou shalt devote all thy service in Zion; and in this thou shalt have strength" (D&C 24:7). That was indeed Joseph's greatest strength: he was always most effective when laboring to establish Zion in the ways of the Lord—when loving Zion, working for Zion, weeping for Zion, and devoting his entire being and all of his energy to Zion; and the strength of the Lord always failed him when he left his labors in Zion and tried to do the world's work. "Be patient in afflictions," the Lord instructed him, "for thou shalt have many; but endure them, for . . . I am with thee" (D&C 24:8). His work was clearly to establish and confirm the Church in the gospel. But "in temporal labors thou shalt not have strength," he was told rather bluntly, "for this is not thy calling" (D&C 24:9). Have we somehow overlooked the significance of *that* important statement? Joseph Smith was plainly called to labor for Zion, not to do the work of the world: he was, after all, a mediocre politician, an ineffective militarist, and a lousy banker;[8] and the cities he established have survived only as visitors' centers and tourist traps, whereas the colonies founded by Brigham Young, who had a very different calling, are thriving communities today. The Lord therefore gave Joseph specific instructions, saying: "Attend to thy calling and thou shalt have wherewith to magnify thine office" (D&C 24:9). And once again we see the nature of his calling and his office: he was chosen to perform the theological function of revealing the Book of Mormon to a lost and fallen world as the doctrinal standard of the Restoration; he was called as a minister of the gospel to perform the ecclesiastical function of reconstituting Zion on earth; and his office was to restore the gospel to the world through the Church. Thus, he was promised everything necessary for magnifying his office if he would only attend to his calling; and both functions of his calling were emphasized, for he was explicitly instructed "to expound all scriptures," which constitutes his doctrinal or theological function, and to "continue in laying on of the hands and confirming the churches" (D&C 24:9), which constitutes his ecclesiastical function. And finally, in a terse remark that should give pause to anyone who understands the Prophet's calling, the Lord said to him: "Thou art called to prune my vineyard with a mighty pruning, yea, even for the last time" (D&C 24:19). Now *that* is an important statement. Joseph Smith was verily required to prune the Lord's vineyard; and everyone he ordained, and all other stewards of the church, were to assist him in doing it. The Lord's vineyard includes, to be sure, the strengths and weaknesses of the true church; but it subsumes much more than that, for it also includes the "Christian" churches, with all of their corruptions and problems, as well as the world at large. The importance of this pruning, moreover, is discussed throughout the Doctrine and Covenants (D&C 39:13–17; 75:2; 88:70–75; and 95:4, for example).[9] "It is the eleventh hour, and the last time that I shall call laborers into my vineyard. And my vineyard has become corrupted every whit; and there is none which doeth good save it be a few; and they err in many instances because of priestcrafts, all having corrupt minds. And verily, verily, I say unto you, that this church have I established and called forth out of the wilderness. And even so will I gather mine elect from the four quarters of the earth, even as many as will believe in me, and hearken unto my voice" (D&C 33:3–6). That process has occurred in part, is still occurring, and will occur in the future. Since the Lord's vineyard had been thoroughly corrupted, Joseph had to recultivate it with redemptive machinery, bring the Church "out of obscurity and out of darkness" (D&C 1:30) in order to do it, and call laborers to the pruning; and they have never left the vineyard, for the work begun by Joseph Smith continues to this day.

Two years earlier, after losing a lengthy manuscript from the "Book of Lehi"[10] by giving something less than complete devotion to the will of the Lord and loaning it to a "friend," Joseph was confronted with harsh words from the heavens. Before reviewing this stinging reprimand, however, I invite you, dear reader, to assume the role of Joseph Smith by standing in his shoes, so to speak, as though you were the prophet and this were an actual revelation from the Lord, in person, to you. How would you feel if the Lord told *you* the following because you had bungled the work you were called to do?

> The works, and the designs, and the purposes of God cannot be frustrated, neither can they come to naught.
>
> For God doth not walk in crooked paths, neither doth he turn to the right hand nor to the left, neither doth he vary from that which he hath said; therefore, his paths are straight, and his course is one eternal round.
>
> Remember, remember that it is not the work of God that is frustrated, but the work of men;
>
> For although a man may have many revelations, and have power to do many mighty works, yet if he boasts in his own strength, and sets at naught the counsels of God, and follows after the dictates of his own will and carnal desires, he must fall and incur the vengeance of a just God upon him.
>
> Behold, you have been entrusted with these things, but how strict were your commandments; and remember also the promises which were made to you, if you did not transgress them.
>
> And behold, how oft you have transgressed the commandments and the laws of God, and have gone on in the persuasions of men.
>
> For behold, you should not have feared man more than God. Although men set at naught the counsels of God, and despise his words—
>
> Yet you should have been faithful; and he would have extended his arm and supported you against all the fiery darts of the adversary; and he would have been with you in every time of trouble.
>
> Behold, thou art Joseph, and thou wast chosen to do the work of the Lord; but because of transgression, if thou art not aware thou wilt fall.
>
> But remember, God is merciful; therefore, repent of that which thou hast done which is contrary to the commandment which I gave you, and thou art still chosen, and art again called to the work;
>
> Except thou do this, thou shalt be delivered up and become as other men, and have no more gift. . . .
>
> And this is the reason that thou hast lost thy privileges for a season—For thou hast suffered the counsel of thy director to be trampled upon from the beginning (D&C 3:1-11, 14-15; section 10 should also be consulted in its entirety).

How would you like to be addressed that way by the Lord? He is saying to the Prophet in effect: "Now see here, Joseph—enough is enough! My work will go on, with you or without you! If you don't repent of your sins this instant, so you can again be called to the work, others will take your place; but get this through your head, if you can: *my work will go on!*" The Lord then tells Joseph in great plainness that the gospel must go forth to all the world—not only to Jews and Gentiles but also to the descendants of Joseph, his namesake, who was sold into Egypt—and reminds him in forceful terms that the unnecessary loss of this important manuscript had interrupted the work of redemption. "Nevertheless, my work shall go forth, for inasmuch as the knowledge of a Savior has come unto the world, through the testimony of the Jews, even so shall the knowledge of a Savior come unto . . . the Nephites . . . through the testimony of their fathers—and this testimony shall come to the knowledge of the Lamanites . . . who dwindled in unbelief because of the iniquity of their fathers. . . . And for this very purpose are these plates preserved, which contain these records—that the promises of the Lord might be fulfilled, which he made to his people; . . . and that they might know the promises of the Lord, and . . . believe the gospel and rely upon the merits of Jesus Christ, and be glorified through faith in his name, and that through their repentance they might be saved" (D&C 3:16–20).[11]

The Prophet was thus rebuked from time to time for failing to take the Lord's work of redemption more seriously than anything else. Joseph Smith, in a word, was a sinner, "for all have sinned, and come short of the glory of God" (Rom. 3:23);[12] but he was not an unrepentant sinner: he was a self-conscious, confessing sinner who turned to the Lord in a spirit of profound contrition, brokenhearted for his sins, seeking the mercy and forgiveness of God, and repenting for all he was worth. And the Lord loved him and accepted his repentance and remitted his sins and called him back to the work from which he had departed. Joseph once told the Latter-day Saints: "Search your hearts, and see if you are like God. I have searched mine, and feel to repent of all my sins."[13] And we should follow his counsel.

All of this is closely related to another problem. There is a basic difference between the gospel and the Church: they constitute separate entities that are intimately related, to be sure; but Joseph Smith was called to restore *both* of them, and they are never identified or confused with each other in the scriptures. Four years before obtaining the Book of Mormon, Joseph learned from Moroni that "the fulness of the everlasting gospel was contained in it;"[14] and the Doctrine and Covenants later confirmed repeatedly that the Book of Mormon indeed contains "the fulness of the gospel" (D&C 20:89; see also sections 27:5; 42:12; 135:3; cf. 3 Nephi 27:13–21). That always confuses those who equate the gospel with the Church; for if the Book of Mormon contains the fulness of the gospel, why doesn't it discuss things like premortal life, the Word of Wisdom, salvation for the dead, eternal progression, the welfare plan, temple marriage, exaltation, or the three degrees of glory? Why are so many of these things not even mentioned in the Book of Mormon if it contains the fulness of the gospel? What *is* the fulness of the gospel, anyway? Well, the Book of Mormon does discuss the gospel, which is the main concern of the Church; but the fulness of the gospel is obviously not the fulness of truth. Our missionaries, who are called to bear witness of the gospel, testify that the Book of Mormon "contains the truth and the word of God,"[15] but no one can reasonably argue that the Book of Mormon contains all truth. The gospel, which is fully contained in the Book of Mormon, is a unique and special kind of truth: it is redemptive truth — the truth, the whole truth, and nothing but the truth about man's redemption from his lost and fallen state. It therefore constitutes the most important truth there is; and it is exactly the kind of truth that the world has always rejected. But the gospel does not include *all* truth, and the puerile notion that it does, despite its popularity in the Church today, can be traced to platonists like Clement of Alexandria, whose guiding maxim was "All truth belongs to the Gospel."[16] But scholars like Clement, both in and out of the Church, have always naturalized the supernatural gospel by reconstructing it along secular lines in order to accept it on their own terms; and they "will not admit that there can be more than one kind of inspiration" — namely, theirs.[17] As Hugh Nibley observes, however, "the Saints have always known better.... We cannot agree with the Talmudist who says that any opinion expressed by a clever scholar is to be received exactly as if it were the word of God to Moses on Sinai — they are not the same at all.... Nor can we agree with the popular academic platitude that since the gospel contains all truth, whatever is taught anywhere, provided only [that] it is true, is the gospel.... All knowledge does come, as Brigham Young assures us, by a kind of revelation, but the idea that all things are equally holy, provided only that they are true, is a cheap and easy fallacy that would be the ruin of any science or discipline.... The man who makes his own mental processes the equivalent of revelation [from heaven] is straining at a very little gnat, while he swallows a camel."[18]

The Book of Mormon, accordingly, contains the fulness of the gospel; but it does not contain the fulness of truth. It cannot provide solutions for the myriad problems of all the secular disciplines, although it reveals the principles of righteousness that should obtain even there. It would be an atrocious text for teaching in most academic or professional fields, since it is not directly concerned with the kinds of temporal truth required for teaching secular subject matters: it would therefore be useless, or very nearly so, for teaching the speculative principles, theories, and critical uses of disciplines like journalism, geophysics, medicine, economics, botany, the fine and useful arts, microbiology, engineering, architecture, acoustics, or chemistry. But the fulness of the everlasting gospel — the whole drama of redemption — *is* presented in the Book of Mormon, which faithfully supplies the eternal truths of revealed religion that are systematically excluded from the natural "religion of culture"[19] in the West. That is essentially what the Lord told Oliver Cowdery, who "wrote" large portions of the Book of Mormon as Joseph's scribe:[20] "Behold, I have manifested unto you, *by my Spirit* . . . that the things which you have written are true; wherefore you know that they are true. And if you know [*by revelation*] that they are true, . . . I give unto you a commandment, that you rely upon the things which are written; for in them are all things written concerning the foundation of my church, my gospel, and my rock" (D&C 18:2–4; emphasis added).

It is not widely known that "the most enlightened Greeks and Romans were all initiates to the Mysteries" of revealed religion because "all of their writings that have reached us have been screened by rationalistic pagan and Christian schoolmen."[21] The biblical writings all went through the selfsame desacralizing process with the help of Jewish scholarship, since the schools of antiquity, like their Darwinian reincarnations, went far beyond the reformations that preceded them and "took over aggressively and eagerly, completely supplanting their Mantic predecessors."[22] This takeover is the direct result of metaphysical naturalism, the learned worldview of high antiquity that controlled the Greco-Roman cultures and still controls all forms of Western education.

We ourselves, whether we like it or not, are the heirs of the Greeks and Romans.... In a thousand different ways, they are permanently and indestructibly woven into the fabric of our own existences. This has been occasionally questioned ... [by] increased knowledge of other ancient civilizations.... It is now clear how much more the Greeks themselves owed to near-eastern civilizations than we had thought.... But *it is through the Greeks that these near-eastern elements have been filtered through to us,* and ... the Greco-Roman contribution to our own ways of living and thinking is not diminished by such knowledge. Without that massive contribution we should not be what we are [today]. Its influences crowd in upon us ... at every level of consciousness.... The Greeks and Romans lived through ... events and developments ... which prefigured and prompted what has ... happened, what is still happening, and what will happen in the future, to our own lives and ... communities.[23]

A recent flap over the Dead Sea Scrolls, to cite a current example, has arisen because the actual documents buried at Qumran have been recovered without undergoing the extensive copying and recopying processes controlled by Western schoolmen. The scrolls are thus too "Christian" for Jewish scholars, too "Jewish" for Christian scholars (since they undermine the supposed "originality" of Christianity), and "too much" for pagan scholars. And since this secular editing process has removed the plain and precious truths of revealed religion from virtually all documents surviving from antiquity, any serious attempt to create an authentic Latter-day Saint education must acknowledge that formidable problem and incorporate into itself the restoration of these revealed truths through the work of Joseph Smith. "We must [therefore] be willing," says President Kimball, "to break with the educational establishment [if necessary], not foolishly or cavalierly, but thoughtfully and for good reason," in order to do things like this.[24]

Whereas secular religions of culture lack the gospel itself, accordingly, there is nothing essential to the gospel that is missing from the Book of Mormon: it is the most Christ-loving book in existence; and though it doesn't cover everything, it *does* contain everything we need to know about the Fall of man, which describes the existential predicament of the human race, and the Atonement of Christ, which provides the only means of redeeming human beings from their lost and fallen predicament. That is the truth of the gospel, and the Book of Mormon contains it fully. The whole drama of redemption from death and sin, which presupposes the actual Fall of all mankind and the infinite Atonement of Jesus Christ, is presented in the Book of Mormon precisely because it contains the fulness of truth about the gospel—not about everything *except* the gospel. That explains why the Book of Mormon is the very best means available to the Church for converting people to the gospel. "Take away the Book of Mormon and the revelations," says Joseph Smith, "and where is our religion? We have none."[25] And why must *that* be so? It's because the revealed witness of Jesus Christ, which the Holy Ghost confirms to anyone who has personal knowledge of the Book of Mormon and faith unto repentance, is the key to everything of worth in our religion. Without that witness, needless to say, the Book of Mormon is nothing but paper and ink: it's only black marks on a white background unless the Spirit of the Lord brings it to life in the hearts and minds of its readers; and reading it is just like reading any other book unless the Holy Ghost informs the reading. The Book of Mormon is thus like everything else in the kingdom: the missionaries, the scriptures, the programs of the Church, anything said or done by any of its stewards (including the visits of home teachers, the labors of stake presidents and bishops, the speeches of the Brethren and their travels around the world, and even the Church itself)—these things count for little if anything unless they function as vehicles of revelation, since the kingdom itself and all of its resources serve only as the means of bringing people in our world into actual contact with the redeeming power of God's world. Once contact is made, however, we must decide whether we accept it and want more contact because we like its influence, or reject it and want no further contact because we dislike its influence. If we like its influence, of course, we will renew its presence in our lives by seeking it through the scriptures and other resources of the Church; and we will labor willingly in the kingdom because its resources are essential for the redemption of Zion. But if we dislike its influence in our lives, if we turn away from it because it scares us to death, or if we want nothing further to do with it for any reason, then the Church, the Brethren, the missionaries, and the scriptures reduce to zero significance—they don't mean a thing.[26] That, furthermore, is exactly as it should be, for these things are only redemptive instruments. The machinery of redemption was designed by God as his means of introducing people to the realities of a better world, and by doing that, to secure the redemption of anyone who wants to be redeemed. It cannot redeem anybody else.[27]

The twentieth section of the Doctrine and Covenants presents this same picture of the Book of Mormon. "After it was truly manifested unto [Joseph Smith] . . . that he had received a remission of his sins, he was entangled again in the vanities of the world; but after repenting, and humbling himself sincerely, through faith, God ministered unto him by an holy angel . . . and gave him power from on high . . . to translate the Book of Mormon; which contains a record of a fallen people, and the fulness of the gospel of Jesus Christ" (D&C 20:5-6, 8-9).

Here again, the doctrines of the Fall and the Atonement characterize the message of the Book of Mormon, which verifies the biblical account of man's fallen nature and the human need of redemption: it regards all mankind as lost and fallen; but it also shows that "the way is prepared from the fall of man" (2 Ne. 2:4) and bids us take it. The Nephites, Lamanites, and Jaredites, accordingly, were lost and fallen people, even as we are; and their scriptural record was designed to bring the fulness of the gospel into the otherwise hollow existence of human beings. "By these things we know that there is a God in heaven . . . [who] created man, male and female, after his own image and in his own likeness . . . and gave unto them commandments that they should love and serve him, the only living and true God, and that he should be the only being whom they should worship" (D&C 20:17-19). These three directives constitute everything required of Adam and Eve — to love God, to serve God, and to worship God alone; and they are essentially all that is required of us. But neither they nor we have been able to do that, for "by the transgression of these holy laws man became sensual and devilish, and became fallen man" (D&C 20:20); and once our first parents had fallen, they transmitted their fallen nature to their children and ultimately to us. If we kept all of God's commandments, if we really *did* that, he would not need to provide an atonement for our sins because we would not be sinful. But God gives commandments and people break them; and thus our need of redemption is absolute: there is no salvation for anyone without a Redeemer who is fully capable of saving us from death and sin. "Wherefore, the Almighty God gave his Only Begotten Son, as it is written in those scriptures which have been given of him. He suffered temptations but gave no heed unto them. He was crucified, died, and rose again the third day; and ascended into heaven, to sit down on the right hand of the Father, to reign with almighty power according to the will of the Father; that as many as would believe and be baptized in his holy name, and endure in faith to the end, should be saved" (D&C 20:21–25).

This states the conditions of redemption for everybody. We know, therefore, "that all men must repent and believe on the name of Jesus Christ, and worship the Father in his name, and endure in faith on his name to the end, or they cannot be saved in the kingdom of God" (D&C 20:29). It is redemptive information of this kind, which covers every aspect of the gospel, that is contained in the Book of Mormon. That is the point made by the Doctrine and Covenants when it says repeatedly that the Book of Mormon contains the fulness of the gospel: it does not mean that the Book of Mormon contains all truth about everything—it means only that the Book of Mormon contains all truth about the gospel; and it does in fact do that.

The gospel is the foundation of revealed religion, and the Church is its superstructure. Since that relationship cannot be inverted without distorting the whole plan of redemption, those who exalt the Church above the gospel are simply wrong—they have built the basement on top of their house. "If it so be that the church is built upon my gospel," said the Lord anciently, "then will the Father show forth his own works in it. But if it be not built upon my gospel," men will "have joy in their works for a season, and by and by the end cometh, and they are hewn down and cast into the fire, from whence there is no return" (3 Ne. 27:10–11). It is only "if you shall build up my church, upon the foundation of my gospel and my rock," as the Lord said before his modern Church was organized, that "the gates of hell shall not prevail against you" (D&C 18:5). If the Church is not based squarely upon the gospel, accordingly, it is not the Lord's Church. Thus, it does not become the Latter-day Saints to give primary allegiance to the Church and only secondary allegiance to the gospel. It's the other way around: we must be faithful above all else to the gospel of our Lord and Savior Jesus Christ; and there is something very wrong with our loyalty to the Church if it is not derived from that. "He that hath the bride," remember, "is the bridegroom" (John 3:29); and if we are truly loyal to the Church, it is because we are faithful to Christ as the redeemer of his bride, and because our faith in the bridegroom creates in us a strong secondary loyalty to the Church as the bride of Christ.

We will never get our thinking straight about religion unless we actually hear and accept the gospel message of *redemption* as it is revealed to us by God. The Saints have therefore been warned to beware concerning themselves, and "to give diligent heed to the words of eternal life" (D&C 84:43). This warning is couched in three messages:

> *Message One* — "The word of the Lord is truth, and whatsoever is truth is light, and whatsoever is light is . . . the Spirit of Jesus Christ" (D&C 84:45).
>
> *Message Two* — "The Spirit [of Jesus Christ] *giveth light* to every man that cometh into the world; and the [same] Spirit [of Jesus Christ] *enlighteneth* every man . . . that hearkeneth to the voice of the Spirit" (D&C 84:46; emphasis added).
>
> *Message Three* — "Every one that hearkeneth to the voice of the Spirit cometh unto God, even the Father. And the Father teacheth him of the covenant which he has renewed and confirmed upon you . . . for the sake of the whole world" (D&C 84:47–48).

The important distinction of D&C 84:46 is virtually never acknowledged by those who think these statements are about "the Light of Christ," which they interpret as something in human nature that functions as an internal verifier of some sort or as the human conscience. But there is a tremendous difference between *giving light "to every man* that cometh into the world," and *enlightening "every man . . . that hearkeneth* to the voice of the Spirit." This difference, moreover, is crucial, since the Spirit of Christ *"enlighteneth"* only those that hearken to the Spirit which enlightens them, whereas the same Spirit of Christ *"giveth light"* unconditionally to every human being. The great importance of this difference is that only those who hearken to the voice of the Spirit come unto God the Father, and that the Father teaches only them about the New and Everlasting Covenant, which he has revealed anew by restoring the gospel and the Church to the world through Joseph Smith. This covenant, which is also known as the Covenant of the Priesthood, is the same fulness of the gospel that constitutes the subject matter of the Book of Mormon: it contains all of the agreements entered into and accepted by the Savior and his Father before the world was — agreements according to which the universe and man have been created and are being redeemed;[28] and it provides for man's participation in the New and Everlasting Covenant through the Oath of the Priesthood (D&C 84:39–40). It can be disquieting, after reading that "the Spirit giveth light to every man that cometh into the world," to learn that the whole world is lost in trespasses and sins. Why, if everyone is lighted by the Spirit of Christ, is everybody sinful? Well, "the Light of Christ" is a doctrine that is not easily understood unless the natural and redemptive functions of the same light are distinguished.[29] But if we make this distinction and reread D&C 84:46, the Spirit clearly "giveth light" to everybody but "enlighteneth" only those who hearken; and this means that the provision of natural light to everyone does not redeem anybody. It is the redemptive function of the Spirit of Christ that redeems us, not its natural function, which only establishes the *possibility* of redemption. Thus, "the whole world lieth in sin, and groaneth under darkness and under the bondage of sin. And by this you may know they are under the bondage of sin, because they come not unto me. For whoso cometh not unto me is under the bondage of sin. . . . And by this you may know the righteous from the wicked, and that the whole world groaneth under sin and darkness even now" (D&C 84:49–51, 53).

That condemns everybody, with only few exceptions,[30] for "light is come into the world, and men loved darkness rather than light, because their deeds were evil" (John 3:19). Good and evil people can thus be distinguished only by their relationship to the Lord: the good come to God through Christ, and the evil do not, "for every one that doeth evil hateth the light, neither cometh to the light, lest his deeds should be reproved. But he that doeth truth cometh to the light, that his deeds may be made manifest" (John 3:20–21). Acceptance or rejection of the light is one of the most important ways we can tell the righteous from the wicked (see D&C 93:31; 1 Jn. 1:57).

The Lord, who thus condemns the world for its sinfulness, also condemns the Church for its worldliness. Because "darkness covereth the earth, and gross darkness the minds of the people," he told his apostles, "all flesh has become corrupt before my face" (D&C 112:23). The world, accordingly, must be cleansed; and the cleansing must commence with his church. "Behold, vengeance cometh speedily upon the inhabitants of the earth, a day of wrath, . . . of burning, . . . of desolation, of weeping, of mourning, and of lamentation; and as a whirlwind it shall come upon all the face of the earth.... And upon my house shall it begin, and from my house shall it go forth ... ; first among those among you, saith the Lord, who have professed to know my name and have not known me, and have blasphemed against me in the midst of my house" (D&C 112:24–26).

This means, of course, that there were unrighteous stewards in the Church in the 1830s; and since they are *always* found in the Church, this early revelation continues to describe many of the Latter-day Saints who are called to stewardships in the Church by the hundreds of thousands along the Wasatch Front and elsewhere. Their zeal for God is often intense, but their ways are not always heavenly ways. This pinpoints a common failing among the "Saints," who have had to learn the hard way that the power of God cannot be utilized for pursuing their own selfish ends because the secular knowledge that enables men to exercise power over *this* world does not govern the powers of heaven. "It is the nature and disposition of almost all men," says Joseph Smith, that "as soon as they get a little authority ... [they] immediately begin to exercise unrighteous dominion," adding that the Latter-day Saints "have learned [this] by sad experience" (D&C 121:39); and he warns the Saints repeatedly about the evils of manipulative thinking, reminding them that if they are called without being chosen it is "because their hearts are set so much on the things of this world ... that they do not learn this one lesson — that ... the powers of heaven cannot be controlled nor handled only upon the principles of righteousness" (D&C 121:34–38). And the Lord himself, finally, puts his finger squarely on the worst sins of the Latter-day Saints. "Your minds in times past have been darkened because of unbelief, and because you have treated lightly the things you have received — which vanity and unbelief have brought the whole church under condemnation. And this condemnation resteth upon the children of Zion, even all" (D&C 84:54–56).

These are the major sins of the Latter-day Saints: we are guilty of unbelief because we do not have the faith we should have; and we are guilty of vanity because we take the wrong things seriously and treat the wrong things lightly. Thus, we worry constantly about our behavioral sins — and neglect the sins of vanity and unbelief that darken our minds and diminish the light of the gospel in our lives. We excel as doers, for we can out-Pharisee the Pharisees when it comes to doing this or that in the Church and feeling "good" about it. But the Lord does not accuse us of behavioral sins: it is the fundamental problem of unbelief, the bewildering lack of faith, that confounds the Latter-day Saints; and make no mistake about it: the sin of unbelief is more basic than the behavioral sins that flourish in its wake. And what about the sins of vanity and of treating lightly the things we have received? *Vanitas*, remember, means "emptiness," the opposite of "fulness." If we forsake the fulness of the gospel to seek the world's vanities it can only be because we take the things of man too seriously and the things of God too lightly. The things we have received from God, moreover, not only include everything restored to us through Joseph Smith but refer explicitly to the Book of Mormon as the heart and soul of the Restoration. This means, among other things, that the Latter-day Saints have never taken the Book of Mormon seriously: we do not take it seriously even today, and herein lies the supreme expression of our vanity. I am reluctant to characterize the Latter-day Saints as vain or as disdaining the gifts of God; but our vanities are known to the Lord, and I cannot bring myself to contradict him on this or on any other point. There's no use citing hundreds of instances that could be interpreted as symptoms of Latter-day Saint vanity, for we find the strongest evidence of sinfulness in our own souls; but this sin tops them all, for treating the Book of Mormon lightly, or worse still, making light of the Book of Mormon, has brought the whole Church under condemnation. "And they shall remain under this condemnation until they repent and remember the new covenant, even the Book of Mormon and the former commandments which I have given them . . . otherwise, there remaineth a scourge and judgment to be poured out upon the children of Zion" (D&C 84:57–58).

That condemnation is permanent, apparently, unless we "repent and remember the new covenant," which is specifically identified with the doctrinal content of the Book of Mormon[31] and with the revelations of the Doctrine and Covenants.[32] The new covenant, of course, is the New and Everlasting Covenant of Redemption, the contractual agreements between the Savior and his Father which create the whole plan of salvation:[33] it is "new" only because it has been revealed anew, for it was established before the world was formed and is literally older than the hills;

and its eternal significance constitutes the subject matter of the Book of Mormon, which is attested to the Church by the Doctrine and Covenants. Joseph Smith was to deliver that sacred subject matter "unto the children of men"; and "this unbelieving and stiffnecked generation," he was told explicitly, "shall have my word through you" (D&C 5:6, 8, 10). The Lord has also told his Church that "the fulness of the gospel" is found "in the Bible and the Book of Mormon" (D&C 42:12),[34] that "there are none that doeth good except those who are ready to receive the fulness of my gospel," and that "I have sent forth the fulness of my gospel by the hand of my servant Joseph" (D&C 35:12, 17). Our choices are therefore clear: if we do not repent and remember the new covenant, or in other words, if we do not take the doctrines and practices of the King and of his Kingdom seriously, "there remaineth a scourge and judgment to be poured out upon the children of Zion" (D&C 84:58). I cannot make choices for other Latter-day Saints; but I believe in my own heart that we are inviting the wrath of God to fall upon us if we do not speedily repent of our vanity and unbelief and remember the Book of Mormon and the Doctrine and Covenants.

The Nauvoo House, of all things, is involved in an interesting way with the vanity and unbelief of the Latter-day Saints. Elaborate directions for its construction were given by the Lord, who ordered it built for housing Joseph and his family and "for the boarding of strangers" (D&C 124:56). It was to be "a delightful habitation for man, and a resting-place for the weary traveler" (D&C 124:60). A quorum was organized to build it, and its members were instructed to provide financing by selling stock in amounts not less than $50 or more than $15,000 per stockholder. Then, after swimming through oceans of particulars about the Nauvoo House,[35] we come upon the following: "Let no man pay stock to the quorum of the Nauvoo House unless he shall be a believer in the Book of Mormon, and [in] the revelations I have given unto you. . . . For that which is more or less than this cometh of evil, and shall be attended with cursings and not blessings, saith the Lord" (D&C 124:119–20).

We are thus told suddenly, and point-blank, that the Lord did not want money from any of the Latter-day Saints under any circumstances for building the Nauvoo House unless they were believers in the Book of Mormon and in the Doctrine and

Covenants. So, what goes on here? Selling stock was necessary, wasn't it? Isn't that the purpose for which the quorum of the Nauvoo House was organized? Why, then, should buying stock in the Nauvoo House involve anyone in evil and elicit curses from the Lord for doing it? Well, the Lord has charged his "Saints" with the sin of unbelief; but they have taken that charge lightly, and he is serious about it. We have talked ourselves into believing that we can *do* everything the Saints of God have always done without having the faith they have always had—that we can observe the *practices* of revealed religion, in other words, without accepting the *principles* of the gospel; and that is blatantly false. The situation regarding the Nauvoo House, furthermore, is fully generalizable, since faith in the King must always precede and generate good works in the kingdom. This principle, accordingly, functions as the criterion for evaluating the actions of any person who does anything at all in the Church. Can we be cursed, then, for going to the welfare farm? According to this we can. When the bishop calls us to do anything in the ward he is supposedly calling people who already have faith in the Lord Jesus Christ and in the prophetic mission of Joseph Smith. If we do things like going to the welfare farm, therefore, or supporting missionaries in the field, it should be because we *believe* in the Savior and in his prophet; and if we do not believe in them, we are in the same boat with those who purchased stock in the Nauvoo House without believing in the Book of Mormon or the Doctrine and Covenants and got cursings instead of blessings for their folly. Now, that is a very scary thing! We are dead wrong if we think we can just do this or that in the Church because our quorum adviser or Relief Society president or bishop or somebody else asks us to do it, and that's all there is to it—that we are not really required to believe in the divine life and mission of Jesus Christ, or the realities of life in this fallen world, or the restoration of the gospel and the kingdom of God through the Prophet Joseph Smith. If we do not believe in these things, then we can indeed be condemned for doing what we do in the Church. Is there any other way to read this? It is crucially important that we believe in these things and repent of our sins before the Lord. The sins of vanity and unbelief that plague the Latter-day Saints are deadly, for they feed the behavioral sins which thrive on them. We must never forget the tragic story of the Nauvoo House: the tragedy is not what became of it, but what the Saints became when they banked on it without believing in the things of God.

Virtually everything we have observed thus far is epitomized in three additional sections of the Doctrine and Covenants. Sections 1 and 20, first of all, provide the following pertinent overview: "I the Lord, knowing the calamity which should come upon the inhabitants of the earth, called upon my servant Joseph Smith, Jun., and spake unto him from heaven, and gave him commandments; and also gave commandments to others, that they should proclaim these things unto the world; . . . that man should not counsel his fellow man, neither trust in the arm of flesh—but that every man might speak in the name of God the Lord, even the Savior of the world; that faith also might increase in the earth; that mine everlasting covenant might be established; [and] that the fulness of my gospel might be proclaimed by the weak and the simple unto the ends of the world" (D&C 1:17-23).

It is important to note that Joseph was not alone in his labors, for working with him in the kingdom were others who received commandments from on high, spoke in the name of the Lord, delivered the message of the Restoration, heralded the New and Everlasting Covenant, proclaimed the fulness of the gospel, and nourished the seedlings of faith in the hearts of men. "Having received the record of the Nephites," therefore, Joseph was able "to translate through the mercy . . . [and] power of God, the Book of Mormon"; and "those to whom these commandments were given" also received "power to lay the foundation of this church, and to bring it forth out of obscurity and out of darkness" (D&C 1:29-30). Joseph was thus assisted not only by scribes like Oliver Cowdery, but by others who solemnly attested the validity of his mission.

> [The Book of Mormon] was given by inspiration, and is confirmed to others by the ministering of angels, and is declared unto the world by them—proving to the world that the holy scriptures are true, and that God does inspire men and call them to his holy work in this age. . . . Therefore, having so great witnesses [to the coming forth of the Book of Mormon], by them shall the world be judged, even as many as shall hereafter come to a knowledge of this work. And those who receive it in faith, and work righteousness, shall receive a crown of eternal life; but those who harden their hearts in unbelief, and reject it, it shall turn to their own condemnation—for the Lord God has spoken it; and we, the elders of the church, have heard and bear witness (D&C 20:10-11, 13-16).

That is a marvelous summary of the Restoration, and D&C 135 contains another one. This section was written by Elder John Taylor after the prophet and his brother were murdered; and it, too, describes the work of Joseph Smith in terms of his theological and ecclesiastical functions, which are directly related to the Book of Mormon and the Doctrine and Covenants.

> To seal the testimony of this book [of Doctrine and Covenants] and the Book of Mormon, we announce the martyrdom of Joseph Smith the Prophet, and Hyrum Smith the Patriarch. They were shot in Carthage jail, on the 27th of June, 1844, . . . by an armed mob — painted black. . . .
>
> Joseph Smith, the Prophet and Seer of the Lord, has done more, save Jesus only, for the salvation of men in this world, than any other man that ever lived in it. In the short space of twenty years, he has brought forth the Book of Mormon, which he translated by the gift and power of God, and has been the means of publishing it on two continents; has sent the fulness of the everlasting gospel, which it contained, to the four quarters of the earth; has brought forth the revelations and commandments which compose this book of Doctrine and Covenants, and many other wise documents and instructions for the benefit of the children of men; . . . and like most of the Lord's anointed in ancient times, has sealed his mission and his works with his own blood; and so has his brother Hyrum. . . .
>
> The testators are now dead, and their testament is in force. . . .
>
> And henceforward their names will be classed among the martyrs of religion; and the reader in every nation will be reminded that the Book of Mormon, and this book of Doctrine and Covenants of the church, cost the best blood of the nineteenth century to bring them forth for the salvation of a ruined world (D&C 135:1, 3, 5-6).

And there we have it: that is what constitutes the work of Joseph Smith. Whatever *else* he did may have its own importance; but by far the most important thing about him is the fact that he was assigned this double mission, the twin tasks of restoring the eternal *principles* of the gospel, which are in the Book of Mormon, and the temporal *practices* of the Church, which are in the Doctrine and Covenants.

This distinction between eternal principles and temporal practices is supremely important for anyone who essays to teach revealed religion by the Spirit of the Lord. It is crucial because "the elders, priests and teachers of this church shall *teach the principles of my gospel*, which are in the Bible and the Book of Mormon, in the which is the fulness of the gospel. And they shall *observe the covenants and church articles to do them*, and these shall be their teachings as they shall be directed by the Spirit" (D&C 42:12–13; emphasis added; cf. D&C 33:14).[36]

Our teachers should be teaching the *principles* of the gospel, in other words, and observing the *practices* of the Church while they are doing it, for they, like "every person who belongeth to this church of Christ, shall observe to keep all the commandments and covenants of the church" (D&C 42:78); those who are taught should do likewise by learning the same principles and observing the same practices; and in this way, "he that preacheth and he that receiveth, understand one another, and both are edified and rejoice together" (D&C 50:22; see D&C 50:13–24 for fuller information about both ends of this inspired teaching-learning process). We are not to teach the *practices* of the Church in isolation, mind you, while ignoring the *principles* of the gospel, although many teachers seem unable to teach in any other way.[37] Remember, saith the Lord to all who teach in his Church, that "the Spirit shall be given unto you by the prayer of faith; and if ye receive not the Spirit ye shall not teach" (D&C 42:14), for revealed religion cannot be taught in any other way.

Thus, the Lord uses a theological account of the Nephite ministry, which he recorded and controlled through ancient prophets, to clarify and explain the fulness of the gospel by retrieving the Book of Mormon from the bowels of the earth as the doctrinal standard of the Restoration; and he also uses the Church as his best means of ensuring that the gospel is properly taught to the children of men. That is what Joseph Smith is all about: the thing about him that really matters is the dual nature of his prophetic mission; and everything else about him is subordinate to this. In the end, perhaps, he said it best himself. After waiting "in Kirtland to be endowed, . . . the elders would go forth, and each must . . . go in all meekness, in sobriety, and preach Jesus Christ and Him crucified; [they are] not to contend with others on account of their faith, but [to] pursue a steady course. This I delivered by way of commandment; and all who observe it not, will pull down persecution upon their heads, while those who do [it], shall always be filled with the Holy Ghost; this I pronounced as a prophecy, and sealed with hosanna and amen."[38]

The prophet also asked and answered a list of twenty questions, which he published in order to avoid "the trouble of repeating the same a thousand times over and over again." The final and most basic question in the list was: "What are the fundamental principles of your religion?" And he gave the following important answer: "The fundamental principles of our religion are the testimony of the Apostles and Prophets concerning Jesus Christ, that He died, was buried, and rose again the third day, and ascended into heaven; and *all other things which pertain to our religion are only appendages to it.*"[39]

We often seem to think that appendages to the gospel are the fundamental realities of our religion—as though by-products of the gospel were more important than the gospel itself! That, of course, is categorically false, for Christ is the vine, we are the branches, and apart from Him we can do nothing (see John 15:1–7); and nothing makes this plainer than the dual nature of the work Joseph Smith was called to do: the principles of the gospel are revealed in the Book of Mormon; and all of the redemptive machinery required for promulgating the gospel was restored when the prophet reestablished the kingdom of God on earth. We must never lose track of these two functions of Joseph's mission: they are what he was *for*, since they constitute the basic elements of the work he was commanded by the Lord to do. And we should take advice from one of his most important sayings: "A fanciful and flowery and heated imagination beware of; because the things of God are of deep import; and time, and experience, and careful and ponderous and solemn thoughts can only find them out. Thy mind, O man! if thou wilt lead a soul unto salvation, must stretch as high as the utmost heavens, and search into and contemplate the darkest abyss, and the broad expanse of eternity—*thou must commune with God.*"[40]

There is a sonnet, finally, that accurately summarizes the work of Joseph Smith. It was written by my oldest son, David, after he returned to BYU from his mission.

## THE WORK OF JOSEPH SMITH
### By David C. Wright

The fulness of the gospel was obscured,
And God remained in heaven, people said;
Till one day revelation was restored,
And then the morning broke, the shadows fled.
In answer to the youthful Joseph's search
Divine commandments from Jehovah came,
To lay the sure foundation of his church,
The fulness of his gospel to proclaim.

For this the Book of Mormon was revealed.
Its message of redemption marks the birth
Of God's concluding harvest in the field,
And pruning in the vineyards of the earth.
Thus, with the Father's witness of his Son,
The final dispensation was begun.[41]

# Notes

1. From the last sentence in the fourth paragraph of the "Explanatory Introduction" to the Doctrine and Covenants, which has no pagination.

2. The Book of Mormon attitude toward history is stated in 1 Nephi 6:1–6; 9:2–4; 19:1–6; 2 Nephi 4:14–15; 5:29–33; and Jacob 1:1–4. These statements are discussed by Boyd K. Packer in the *Ensign*, May 1986, 59–61.

3. Cf. 2 Nephi 5:33: "If my people desire to know the more particular part of the history of my people they must search mine other plates."

4. Joseph's alignment with the Book of Mormon, of course, involves "expounding *all* scriptures unto the church" (D&C 24:5; emphasis added), including his work with the Books of Abraham and Moses, his inspired revisions of Bible texts, and so forth.

5. This sentence was originally intended to discourage my missionary son from discussing with other missionaries the theories of a BYU professor about eternal progression and the King Follett discourse. See below, note 41.

6. I am myself an example of this folly. I have been an avid reader of the scriptures from my youth. I have studied them a lot—a *real* lot—in several languages; but for some reason, which can only be explained as a kind of blindness, I have lived too many of my days without understanding the dual nature of the prophet Joseph's mission as it is explained in the Doctrine and Covenants. I have studied and taught the Book of Mormon at BYU more than I have taught the Doctrine and Covenants; and I acknowledge, too, that I have joshed with teachers of the Doctrine and Covenants over the years, telling them, for example, that I had the advantage over them because the Book of Mormon is discussed at length in the Doctrine and Covenants, whereas the Doctrine and Covenants is not even mentioned in the Book of Mormon—something I have since learned from President Benson is not quite true; see 2 Ne. 13:38–41 and 3 Ne. 27:25–26. I once got a laugh in a faculty meeting, believe it or not, by calling the Doctrine and Covenants "a marvelous soporific" and saying "you can read it when you have insomnia and it will put you to sleep!" That was lighthearted banter, of course, as I truly love the Doctrine and Covenants; and I am chagrined to realize that, for so many

years, I failed completely to understand its solid alignment with the redemp-tive content of Joseph Smith's prophetic mission.

7. See my article, "Ancient Burials of Metal Documents in Stone Boxes — Their Implications for Library History," *Journal of Library History* 16, no. 1 (winter 1981), 48–70. This article was reprinted in Donald G. Davis, ed., *Libraries and Culture* ("Proceedings of Library History Seminar VI," 19–22 March 1980 [Austin: University of Texas Press, 1981]), 48–70, and has been reprinted a second time by the Foundation for Ancient Research and Mormon Studies, catalog no. WRI-81. An expanded version of the article has also appeared as a forty-two-page booklet entitled *Ancient Burials of Metallic Foundation Documents in Stone Boxes* ("Occasional Papers," no. 157, December, 1982; Urbana-Champaign, Ill.: University of Illinois, Graduate School of Library and Information Science, 1983), which has been republished under its original title in John M. Lundquist and Stephen D. Ricks, eds., *By Study and also by Faith: Essays in Honor of Hugh W. Nibley* (Salt Lake City: Deseret Book, 1990), vol. 2, pp. 273–334.

8. Cf. Edward Pessen, *Jacksonian America; Society, Personality, and Politics* (Rev. ed.; Urbana Ill.: University of Illinois Press, 1985), 145–46, who notes that "bank failures were disturbingly common" in the Jacksonian era and de-scribes "the difficulties presented by the circulation of a chaos of currencies, some of them backed by a prayer — as was literally a Mormon bank estab-lished in Ohio in 1837 with hardly any capital — and subject to drastic depreciation."

9. There are also numerous references (like D&C 21:9) to laboring and laborers in the Lord's vineyard in the Doctrine and Covenants.

10. See the heading to section 3 of the Doctrine and Covenants.

11. The term "Nephites" here includes Jacobites, Josephites, and Zoramites, just as "Lamanites" includes Lemuelites and Ishmaelites. Genetic mixtures of all these Book of Mormon peoples occur among their survivors, who are known collectively as "Lamanites" today.

12. "Of course, every human being [including Joseph Smith] is a sinner. No man or woman ever lived on this earth, excepting the Son of God, who was not a sinner. The Presidency of this Church, the Twelve Apostles and all the Prophets that ever lived upon this earth are and have been sinners. It is one of the consequences of the fall. We are [all] subject to sin and temptation," George Q. Cannon, *Gospel Truth: Discourses and Writings of George Q. Cannon*, ed. Jerreld L. Newquist (Salt Lake City: Deseret Book, 1987), 1:127.

13. Joseph Smith, *Teachings of the Prophet Joseph Smith,* comp. Joseph Fielding Smith (Salt Lake City: Deseret Book, 1938), 216.

14. Joseph Smith—History 1:34. Joseph thus learned this important fact about the Book of Mormon on 21 September 1823, four years before the golden plates were given him on 22 September 1827, seven years before the church was organized, and twelve years before there was a Doctrine and Covenants. The Lord also reminded Joseph of this fact in August 1830, saying: "The hour cometh that I will drink of the fruit of the vine with you on the earth, and with Moroni, whom I have sent unto you to reveal the Book of Mormon, containing the fulness of my everlasting gospel" (D&C 27:5).

15. As the Lord told Martin Harris in D&C 19:26.

16. Hugh Nibley, *The World and the Prophets* (Salt Lake City: Deseret Book, 1962), 67.

17. Ibid., 27–28.

18. Ibid., 28.

19. The sophic antigospel, which constitutes the secular traditions of western Europe and elsewhere, is called the "religion of culture" by Charles Norris Cochrane, *Christianity and Classical Culture; a Study of Thought and Action from Augustus to Augustine* (New York: Oxford University Press, 1980), 29.

20. Oliver Cowdery may be compared to J. Reuben Clark Jr., who once quipped that he "wrote" the *Articles of Faith* because he did—as James E. Talmage's secretary.

21. Hugh Nibley, *The Ancient State: The Rulers and the Ruled*, ed. Donald W. Parry and Stephen D. Ricks, "The Collected Works of Hugh Nibley," v. 10 (Salt Lake City: Deseret Book, 1991), 321, adding that "it is indeed remarkable that in all the [ancient] literature we fail to find any derogatory remark or witticism about the Mysteries"—especially since Aristophanes and other comic playwrights were always lampooning Greek "natural" religion from the Athenian stage.

22. Ibid., 405.

23. Michael Grant, *The Founders of the Western World: A History of Greece and Rome* (New York: Charles Scribner's Sons, 1991), 1; emphasis added. "Greece and Rome are uniquely able to help us . . . since not only were they our spiritual ancestors but theirs are the only past civilizations spread out for our detailed inspection all the way from beginning to end—from the birth of the historical west in c. 1000 B.C. until its convulsion, fifteen hundred years later, which led directly into our own world. All of us who look at the Greeks and Romans will . . . [discover] much about the conditions of our own times, and . . . about ourselves," ibid., 2. This is the ubiquitous biased view of Greco-Roman naturalistic spirituality, which sees no value at all in revealed spirituality derived from the ancient Near East.

24. Spencer W. Kimball, "Second Century Address," *BYU Studies*, 16, no. 4 (summer 1976), 453.

25. *History of the Church*, 2:52.

26. I am indebted to Chauncey Riddle for meaningful discussions about the scriptures, and indeed about all resources of the Church, as the *means* of making contact with the other world, and for his remarkable insights into the important decisions that contact imposes upon us.

27. According to Alma 11:40-41, Christ "shall come into the world to redeem his people . . . [and] shall take upon him the transgressions of those who believe on his name; . . . and salvation cometh to none else. Therefore the wicked remain as though there had been no redemption made, except it be the loosing of the bands of death" — which is accomplished solely by the Resurrection.

28. See John Taylor, *Mediation and Atonement* (Salt Lake City: Stevens & Wallis, 1950), 96-97, 106-7, 166-67.

29. The redemptive function of the Spirit of Christ is discussed in section 84 of the Doctrine and Covenants, whereas its natural function is discussed in section 88.

30. The main ones being little children and those who die without law. Both of these special groups, however, are automatically redeemed (without preconditions of faith, repentance, or rebirth) through the Atonement of Christ, not through the absence of sin in human nature. Thus, an angel told King Benjamin, speaking of little children, that "*as in Adam, or by nature, they fall*, even so the blood of Christ atoneth for their sins" (Mosiah 3:16; emphasis added). Thus, little children, who fall "when they begin to grow up" as "sin conceiveth in their hearts," according to Moses 6:55, are pure before God because of the Atonement, not because they are sinless, for the blood of Christ could not atone for their sins if they had no sins to atone for. The same is true of all who are redeemed without preconditions by the Atonement of Christ.

31. This covenant is also identified with the Book of Mormon in D&C 39:11, 66:2, and 133:57.

32. The "former commandments," which I have interpreted as referring to the Doctrine and Covenants, *could* refer to the Bible (which was also given to the Saints by God), or possibly to both the Doctrine and Covenants and the Bible. The most likely reference, I think, is to the Doctrine and Covenants, although I am not sure of that and have no way of resolving this ambiguity with certainty.

33. See note 28, above, and its accompanying text.

34. Cf. the First Vision (1820), in which the prophet was told that the ancient church "had administered the fulness of the gospel," which "was no longer on the earth, paragraph 4 of the "Explanatory Introduction" to the Doctrine and Covenants, which lacks pagination.

35. In more than sixty verses of D&C 124:56–118, plus verses 121–22.

36. It is fairly clear from these and related references in Church history that the covenants and articles of the Church are what we would call "practices" of the Church today.

37. I was taught that way in my youth; and while I have not exactly rebelled against that kind of teaching, I do get tired of it, and it is a large part of the reason why, in teaching Book of Mormon at BYU for over three decades, I have emphasized redemptive principles while observing (and encouraging students to observe) the practices of the Church.

38. Joseph Smith, *Teachings of the Prophet Joseph Smith*, 109.

39. Ibid., 121; emphasis added.

40. Ibid., 137; emphasis added.

41. This paper has been edited from a cassette tape I recorded during the first week of February 1981 for David, who was then a missionary in Taiwan. Some of the elders were having heavy discussions about a paper on eternal progression and the King Follett discourse by a BYU professor, and David had written me for information on these subjects. I made the tape in order to discourage him from speculations of this kind, and to emphasize what I felt was essential for a missionary to know about Joseph Smith.

David wrote this sonnet in a paper for a Book of Mormon class he took from me at BYU after returning from his mission. I had made an assignment from the tape I recorded for him which required students (1) to read everything the Doctrine and Covenants says about the Book of Mormon in sections 1:17–33; 18:15; 19:26–27; 20:5–36; 24:1–9,13–19; 27:5–14; 33:4–16; 42:11–17; 84:43–59; 124:56–122; and 135:1–7, (2) to "listen to a discussion of this material, entitled The Work of Joseph Smith, which I recorded for my missionary son in Taiwan some time ago," and (3) to write a one-page paper on the subject: "Why, according to the Doctrine and Covenants, did the Lord reveal the Book of Mormon?" David, of course, had an advantage over other students in the class, since he knew far better than they what I hoped would come of this assignment. Nevertheless, in the unbiased, objective judgment of his doting father, he wrote me one of the finest papers I have ever received from a student in any Book of Mormon class. I was simply stunned, needless to say, by this sonnet, which accurately summarizes the basic elements in the picture of the Book of Mormon presented by the Doctrine and Covenants without succumbing to the tyranny of form.

## Message Three

# Brigham Young and the Natural Man

*Reading Professor H. Curtis Wright's essay entitled "Brigham Young and the Natural Man" is a rewarding experience to persons interested in theology or philosophy. It tackles head-on a fundamental concept about man that is basic to the gospel of Jesus Christ and also to human philosophy.*

*I have known Professor Wright for half a century and oft noted that he has a magnificent obsession for things scriptural, theological, and philosophical. In this essay he works all three. His particular background of languages, secular philosophy, and scripture, combined with an acute and analytical mind, accompanied by a spirit-borne testimony of the gospel of Jesus Christ, qualify him to produce such an essay. Wright demonstrates a valuable gift to be able to comprehend detailed and extensive sources and restate them in understandable summaries.*

*Professor Wright's familiarity with Greek and Latin enables him to discuss word origins and meanings. His astute familiarity with scripture, particularly the Book of Mormon and the writings of Paul, and also his familiarity with the teachings of President Young, prompt him to write with uncommon assurance and intensity.*

*This essay discusses the difficulty of trying to communicate spiritual concepts, using the shortcomings and imperfections of a secular language, and also the impossibility of understanding such concepts without the intervention of the Holy Spirit. Further, Wright demonstrates the likelihood for error and misunderstanding if one reads only fragments of scripture, or isolated bits of Brigham Young by proof texting without close attention to context. In addition, he shows that it is necessary to view man's mortal fallen condition against the wider background of man's entire existence or essence. This is a major and necessary point that he makes if one is to harmonize what otherwise appear to be contradictory positions.*

*Professor Wright's essay is masterful in organization and in content, leading the reader to see theological harmony in the teachings of President Young, Paul, King Benjamin, and the brother of Jared.*

*A word of caution: this essay is not easy reading for most people, but it is well worth the effort required. The most difficult is the first third, after which the argument moves more quickly through the remaining pages of delightful quotations, occasional humor, a touch of polite sarcasm, and final conclusions. Just as there is necessity in dealing with the whole essence of man theologically, so must the reader deal with the whole essay and not with just a part of it. Some may not agree with Professor Wright's conclusions. He is not casual in manner. His words are muscular and are like sharp teeth. Be that as it may, I found the treatise challenging, informative, and convincing, and recommend it to anyone who desires a deeper understanding of the "natural" man.*

*Robert J. Matthews*
*Dean of Religious Education, 1981–90*
*Brigham Young University*

Brigham Young's understanding of the natural man was not constructed from statements about the nature of man by Nephites or Jaredites like Enos, Benjamin, Abinadi, Ammon, Alma, and the brother of Jared:[1] it was derived from his New England and European backgrounds and refined by latter-day revelation; and for all his spirited defenses of the Book of Mormon against its critics, his self-acknowledged neglect of its theology is strangely apparent to anyone who studies his uses of scripture. He was, of course, a great proponent of the Book of Mormon; but he was not a great expounder of its doctrines, for Brigham Young, in a word, did not come foursquare out of the Book of Mormon. "With us," he told the Saints in 1862, "the Bible is the *first* book, the Book of Mormon comes *next; then* the revelations in the Doctrine and Covenants, [and] *then* the teachings of the living oracles."[2] And less than five years before his death he told the Saints: "I was brought up a Christian, very strictly, and was taught to read the Bible; consequently it is natural for me to believe it—it is according to my traditions, and also from the spirit of revelation from God unto myself. *In all my teachings, I have taught the Gospel from the Old and New Testaments.* I found therein every doctrine, and the proof of every doctrine, the Latter-day Saints believe in, as far as I know. *Therefore I do not refer to the Book of Mormon as often as I otherwise should.*"[3]

For these if for no other reasons, it seems advisable to obtain some understanding of ancient Eurasian beliefs about the *Naturmensch* before trying to understand the Latter-day Saint concept of man, Brigham Young's attitudes toward the natural man, or the implications of total depravity for the Latter-day Saints. But that task, although rewarding, is also formidable because "nature is perhaps [and may actually be] the most complex word in the [English] language."[4] This is the conclusion of a Cambridge scholar, who, after studying "comparable ideas" such as "culture, society, individual, class, art, [and] tragedy," finds that "difficult as all those ideas are, the idea of nature makes them all seem comparatively simple."[5] This apparently innocuous idea has generated "major categories of meaning that have informed Western thought about nature since ancient times." And since Curtius had already isolated in the 1930s at least "fourteen ways in which a single aspect of nature, its personification as the goddess Natura, operated in Latin allegorical poetry alone,"[6] it would seem not only appropriate but *necessary* to observe its influence in ancient Christianity and to remark its presence in the restored gospel before examining its impact on the thought of Brigham Young.

## I. The Carnal, the Natural, and the Spiritual Man

The literature of early Christianity distinguishes sharply between the carnal man, the natural man, and the spiritual man. "The whole man," according to Irenaeus, is tripartite, since he "consists of a fleshly body, a natural spirit, and a revealed spirit."[7] Thus, "all of the redeemed will be resurrected unto [eternal] life possessing their own physical bodies, their own natural spirits, and their own revealed spiritualities."[8] But those who are raised unto eternal punishment will possess only "their own natural spirits and their own physical bodies, in which they exist without the grace of God"[9] during their mortal lives because they reject revelation. There is, for them, no Spirit of God that descends upon anyone from above, no spirituality that God reveals to anybody, and no redeeming witness communicated by God to any of his children that testifies of his Son as the only Savior of mankind. This neglected tripartition of man, so prominent in early Christianity, was also discussed by later writers like Origenes (for whom "man consists of a body, a natural spirit, and a revealed spirituality"[10]), Apollinarius Laodicenus (for whom "man's three parts are a revealed spirituality, a natural spirit, and a body"[11]), and Procopius Gazaeus (for whom scriptural writers likewise affirm "that man consists of . . . his body, his natural spirit, and his revealed spirituality"[12]).

Jude, speaking for the prophets, told the early Church that "people with natural spirits who do not have a revealed spirituality are the hairsplitters"[13] whose subtle distinctions, philosophic niceties, and intellectual divisiveness have subverted believers of all ages. He was thus warning Christians everywhere about the natural man, who shares the natural order with the carnal man and the spiritual man and cannot be understood apart from them. But secularized thinkers of all ages, whether in or outside of the Church, have found it difficult to acknowledge any spirituality except their own. The secularizing tendency of westernized Christianity, moreover, has been to identify the natural man with the carnal man by accepting Plato's condemnation of everything physical, including the human body, as permanently evil. It is therefore essential, in defining the natural man,[14] to understand him as distinct and separate from both the carnal man[15] and the spiritual man.[16] There are literally scores of late Greek and Latin sources that deal with this early Christian tripartition of humanity into carnal, natural, and spiritual components.[17] Its implications cannot be secularized or ignored without distorting beyond recognition revealed information about the natural man.[18]

The carnal man comprises the whole physical dimension of man's tripartite constitition. He is not like the natural man, who lives on earth and according to nature in all kinds of cultural "weather" created by the human spirit. Nor is he like the spiritual man, who also lives on earth but *not* according to nature: he constantly evaluates cultural influences, regarding some as beneficial and others as unwholesome; and he sees the natural order as not only lost and fallen but defined and dominated by the human spirit, whereas he prefers the spirit of God because it connects him by supernatural revelation to a transcendent spirit-world through redemptive faith. The carnal man, accordingly, pertains only to the empirical aspect of man as a physical organism operating by instinct within the natural order. He is the easiest of these three men to understand because he is at least similar, and in some ways virtually identical, in *the natural religion of secular culture* derived from Greco-Roman antiquity and *the prophetic culture of revealed religion* derived from the ancient Near East. It need only be said that the carnal man is not the best of news in either religion, although he fares better in Mormonism than in orthodox Christianity, which was formulated in the platonistic climate of ancient Alexandria.

The word "carnal" derives from *carn-*, the Latin stem of *caro*, which means "flesh." It refers to "meat," the stuff that's wrapped around our bones. The carnal man is simply the man of flesh who lives in the natural universe without involvement in a hypernormal overworld of any kind; and in Plato, the popular version of everything goes with him. The carnal man, accordingly, is not "spiritual" in either the classical or the Christian sense of the word; and that excludes him from both kinds of spirituality. That's also the point, for European history is a jumbled compound of conflicting oriental and occidental spiritualities that scrambles *two* versions of spirituality and *two* kinds of spiritual man[19] — *the revelatory version of redemptive spirituality*, which derives its spiritual man from the supernatural order and his spirituality from a supernatural deity, and *the secular version of natural spirituality*, which derives its natural man from the natural order and his spirituality from the *saeculum*.[20] The carnal man and his lack of spirituality is therefore easily distinguished from either version of the spiritual man; and the real problem is thus to distinguish "the natural man" from "the spiritual man," since the natural man is every whit as "spiritual" in the secular sense of that word as the spiritual man is in its revelatory sense.[21]

Our modern failure to regard carnality, natural spirituality, and revealed spirituality as distinct and separate aspects of the human being accounts for spiritual ambiguities that permeate every Western culture. We have nothing but trouble with this word "spiritual": we run into it all the time, for we are constantly referring to spiritual things that are purely secular and have nothing to do with revealed religion. Without exception, for example, all colleges of humanities and fine arts in every one of our western European universities are based upon the study of the human spirit; and sophisticated expressions of the human spirit in the arts, literature, and philosophy constitute precisely what is studied in those colleges. We are always talking, furthermore, about such things as the Olympic spirit, the spirit of the nineties, the scientific spirit, the *Zeitgeist* [spirit of the times], the corporate spirit, the competitive spirit, the spirit of compromise, the professional spirit, the cooperative spirit, the spirit of a novel (play, concert, speech, movie, country dance, or sporting event), mob spirits, the spirits of war and peace, reforming spirits, spirited horses or people, bottled spirits, etc. None of this has anything to do with actual revelation, since we are definitely involved, like it or not, with *two* kinds of spirituality derived from distinct and separate sources that are rarely differentiated and easily confused: our horizontal spirituality comes from the immanent spirit of naturalism through the Greco-Roman tradition of occidental Europe, whereas our vertical spirituality comes into Europe from the transcendent spirit of redemptivism through the Egypto-Mesopotamian cultures of western Asia. We should therefore observe carefully how we actually use the word "spiritual," since the spiritual man is a very different thing in revelatory than in secular thinking; and because of that difference, there are *two* basic words for "spirit" in both Greek and Latin. The two Greek words, which surface in English as "psyche" and "pneuma," translate into Latin as *anima* and *spiritus*. Thus, the Greek word for the secular spirit is *psyche*,[22] which appears in English words like "psyche," "psychic," "psychology," and "psychosomatic"; and it is paralleled by *pneuma*,[23] the Greek word for the spirit of revealed Christianity.[24] When Jerome translated the Greek New Testament into Latin, accordingly, *psyche* emerged as *anima*, since each of those words denotes the secular spirit of man; and *pneuma* became *spiritus* because both of these words refer to the revealed spirit of God. Like *psyche*, incidentally, *anima* also appears in such English words as "animal," "animate," and "animus"; for it, too, indexes the spiritual or animating principle of natural life. *Animalis*, as a matter of fact, is a Latin adjective meaning "spiritual," which refers, like its Greek correlate *psychikos*, to the spirit of secularism, just as the Christian spirit is translated from the Greek *pneuma* into the Latin *spiritus*. That's why we never hear priests saying "*anima sancta*" if we listen to the mass; but we do hear them chanting "*spiritu sanctu,*" even if we don't know Latin. *Spiritus* is therefore the Christian word for "spirit" in Latin, just as *pneuma* is in Greek, whereas the secular word for "spirit" is *psyche* in Greek and *anima* in Latin.

Paul discloses the implications of these conflicting spiritualities in a letter to the Corinthians. His Greek term *psychikos anthropos* consists of two Greek words translated by the Latin term *animalis homo* and by the English term "natural man" (1 Cor. 2:14); and all three terms, believe it or not, mean "spiritual man."[25] *Psychikos* means "having characteristics or properties of the *psyche*"; and the English term "natural man," since it is translated from *psychikos anthropos*, refers to man as a spiritual *psyche*, not to man as a physical *soma*. Or, to use the Latin term, *animalis homo* designates man as an *anima* but not as a *corpus*. The "natural man," accordingly, is not man regarded merely as a physical organism, for that is precisely what constitutes the carnal man. Paul is definitely talking about the secular version of the spiritual man, which determines exactly what the natural man is. It is therefore clear that the *psychikos anthropos*, the *animalis homo*, and the "natural man" all refer to anyone in this world — regardless of time, place, age, gender, race, or circumstances — whose spirituality is naturalistic. Paul is saying that there *is* a naturalistic spirituality, and that civilized people, like Greeks or Romans who do not have the gospel, are indeed spiritual people; but their spirituality is naturalistic, not revealed, for theirs is the secularized spirituality that created ancient Greece, came into his world through Rome, and has since come into all civilized institutions of western Europe.

Paul also uses the Greek term *pneumatikos anthropos* in referring to the revealed version of the "spiritual man," which he contrasts with the *psychikos anthropos*, the secular version of the spiritual man. The *pneumatikos anthropos*, which translates into Latin as the *spiritualis homo*,[26] expresses his Christian interpretation of the spiritual man perfectly, since *pneumatikos anthropos* and *spiritualis homo* both refer to anyone whose spirituality is revealed. This reaffirms the necessity of distinguishing between a *naturalistic spirituality* whose source is no higher than the human being, which is what we study as the human arts and sciences, and a *revealed spirituality*, the charismatic gift of heaven whose source is much higher than the human being — something we receive from above as a gracious gift from God by faith in Christ through repentance and rebirth. These two spiritualities, which Paul clearly recognizes, are disclosed by a careful translation of 1 Corinthians 2:12-14, which pays close attention to juxtaposed subtleties that escape notice when translators go solely by words. "We are animated, not by the natural spirit of the cosmos, but by the supernatural Spirit of God that descends upon us from above, so that we may distinguish the revealed gifts of God's free grace [from the provisions of nature]. We speak freely of God's gifts, but not in words that generate instruction from humanly originated wisdom: we use words that communicate information revealed by the Holy Spirit; and we also utilize the Holy Spirit as a criterion for determining what is and is not revealed. But the natural man—anyone whose naturalistic spirituality excludes the supernatural—rejects as absurd all things revealed by the Spirit of God: he is incapable of experiencing such things himself and has no means of evaluating them in others in the absence of revelation."[27]

## II. The Orthodox and Latter-day Saint Concepts of Man

The natural man in the Book of Mormon[28] is identical to the natural man in the New Testament[29] and other scriptures for an important reason: the ancient concept of a natural order, which is widely venerated in secular sources but evaluated as fallen and nonredemptive by all of the prophets, constitutes "the oldest idea in the Western intellectual tradition."[30] That explains why Paul—for whom the natural man, guided only by the fallen spirit of man, can neither know nor accept *anything* revealed by the spirit of God—is in perfect harmony with Benjamin, who insists that, "unless he yields to the enticings of the Holy Spirit, and putteth off the natural man and becometh a saint through the Atonement of Christ the Lord," man is not only "an enemy to God" but "has been from the fall of Adam, and will be forever and ever" (Mosiah 3:19). Before being converted, Paul reminds the Ephesians, "we were children of wrath by nature like the rest of mankind,"[31] thus according with the brother of Jared, who regards no one, not even the best of men, as worthy of the Lord, for "because of the fall our natures have become evil continually" (Ether 3:2); and with Alma, for whom, since the fall of man encompassed everybody, "all mankind . . . had become carnal, sensual, and devilish, by nature" (Alma 42:9–10).

The scriptures plainly teach that the natural order itself, together with everything it contains (including all forms of natural life both human and nonhuman), is fallen. That is nowhere more evident than in the Book of Mormon, but we must take its historicity seriously in order to understand this. We cannot take its historicity seriously, on the other hand, if we ignore its actual provenance—which means that we should study the Book of Mormon within its own historical context as an authentic document from the ancient world;[32] and that makes Latin essential in studying the Book of Mormon for at least three reasons: (1) it has a powerful impact on English; (2) English is the language of a revealed translation for the Book of Mormon; and (3) scholarship cannot go beyond revelation for original sources.[33] Thus, the Latin word *natura* (which means "nature") associates "birth" with the English word "nature" (which means *natura*) because both words stem from *natus* (which means "birth"); and that makes the "nature" of anything refer to its ultimate essence—to the inherent forms, inborn characteristics, or innate properties that are fully present within it upon its birth or entrance into the world. "Nature" and its European relatives, moreover, together with shirttail relatives in other linguistic families, have spawned a vocabulary of nature-words so deeply imbedded in all of the western languages that there is no possible way to root it out of them. It is therefore difficult to interpret the "natural man" in King Benjamin in other than European terms, for he meant precisely what we mean when we discuss the natural man: he was talking about the *psychikos anthropos*, just as Paul was. Benjamin and Paul, furthermore, both say things that affront many people, including some Latter-day Saints, who (like Greco-Roman secularists) deny that nature is fallen and view it optimistically while contending with those who assert (like Judeo-Christian revelationists) that it *is* fallen and see it as nonredemptive. This is the classic standoff between Western naturalism and Near Eastern supernaturalism, which must be understood in order to separate the orthodox concept of total depravity from the Latter-day Saint doctrine of a total fall. By "orthodox," of course, since this kind of surgery requires incisive distinctions, we refer to the three orthodoxies of Judaism, Christianity, and Islam, which were all shaped by the same Greek influence that flowed into western Europe through the university of Alexandria. All three orthodoxies were formed in that way: they were all constructed in the language of temporal reality that came straight out of Greece; and they have since been preoccupied with refurbishing houses already built by rational argumentation. Latter-day Saint doctrine, by way of contrast, is based on continuous revelation; and that raises knotty problems of disparity between the Latter-day Saint and orthodox concepts of man, since the Latter-day Saint concept is founded on eternalism in ways that are not relevant to the orthodox concept. These differing concepts of man must be differentiated *before* being evaluated, for no concept of anything can be properly evaluated unless it has first been closely defined and clearly understood.

Eternalism is always associated with the other world in revelatory thought, but there has never been anything in the secular way of thinking, that is more eternal than this world.[34] The natural universe is therefore regarded in Greek thought as an eternal system of temporal particulars in which the system as a whole is the only eternal thing there is. There never was a time, accordingly, when it did not exist as a whole; but its all-inclusive contents, which include absolutely everything that exists, are embroiled in ceaseless temporal change. The natural universe, on this account, was never created, since it has always existed and contains everything there is; and natural language, which is derived from and has developed within the natural universe, is therefore a time-bound instrument for discussing temporal particulars associated with the world we live in. That forces us, in the absence of an eternal language for discussing eternal things, to use temporal language for discussing both temporal and *eternal* things;[35] and this problem becomes acute in communicating the eternalism implicit in the Latter-day Saint concept of man because one kind of language must do two kinds of work. Natural language, in a word, is securely tied to human temporal existence in the natural order and is not hooked up with eternity.

The Latter-day Saint concept of man, although complex, is often oversimplified, even by Latter-day Saints. There's more to it than saying, for example, that man is a child of God, or that mortal life is a test to see if he will do everything the Lord commands. There is, of course, some truth in this. Naturalists, on the other hand, may *also* call man a child of God. Since their God

# Latter-day Saint and Orthodox Concepts of Man

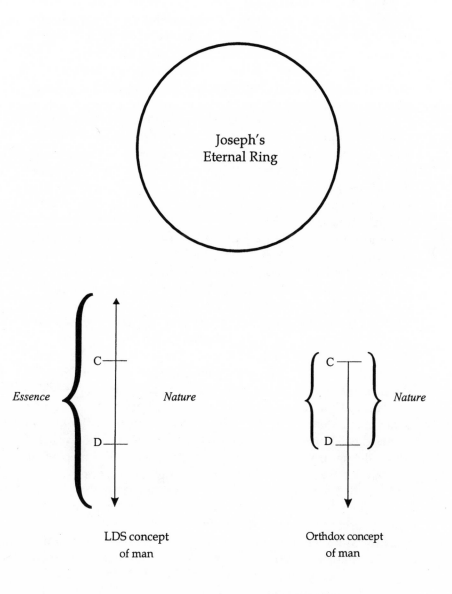

Joseph's
Eternal Ring

Essence

Nature

C

D

LDS concept
of man

C

Nature

D

Orthdox concept
of man

is the natural order, however, they might as well say that men are children of the universe; and they are, in a sense—but it's not the sense in which Latter-day Saints call all men the children of God. It is therefore helpful, in distinguishing the Latter-day Saint from the orthodox concept of man, to begin with Joseph Smith's reference to a ring as the symbol of eternity. Since a ring has no beginning and no end, he says, it symbolizes eternity; but if we cut the ring, it acquires a beginning and an end because cutting it creates a gap in the ring that interrupts its continuity.[36] If we draw a perfect circle, say, three inches in circumference, we can visualize all this by letting the circle stand for Joseph's ring as the symbol of eternity and allowing Joseph's ring to represent the Latter-day Saint concept of man as an eternal being. If we rotate the ring ninety degrees on its vertical axis, it becomes a line three inches high, since we are now looking at the edge of the ring. If we then draw a horizontal mark across the edge of the ring an inch down from the top, and do the same thing an inch up from the bottom, the middle inch defines a gap made in the ring by cutting it in two—a gap that separates the ring from eternity and makes it temporal until it is rejoined.[37] Much of this is suggested, moreover, by English words like "time," "temporary," and "temporal," which are all derived from the Greek verb *temno*,[38] meaning "to cut." So, what have we done? By cutting Joseph's ring, we have separated the temporal aspect of man, which begins with the top side of the cut and ends with its bottom side, from the eternal aspect of man, which has no beginning and no end. The top of the cut now represents man's conception, the earliest point at which the fall of Adam can affect him; and the bottom of the cut represents man's death. It is precisely at this point, accordingly, that Latter-day Saints have their biggest problem with orthodox belief about the nature of man, since premortal eternity has no place in it. Man's conception is thus the beginning of everything: all of a sudden man is there, created out of nothing, just as the universe was created out of nothing. Man therefore moves from conception out of nothing through mortal life to death and into postmortal eternity; and there is no concept whatever of premortal eternity.

The nature of man, for Latter-day Saints, must comprehend their overall concept of man in the totality of his entire existence; and that constitutes an eternal existence out of which and in relation to which man's temporal life is realized, and into which he will return. That obliges us to make a fundamental distinction which the orthodox theologies do not make. This distinction is represented in our diagram by a brace around the right side of the gap in Joseph's severed ring, beginning with the top of the gap, which symbolizes man's conception, and ending with the bottom of the gap, which symbolizes man's death; and the embraced gap itself, which represents the temporal aspect of eternity, symbolizes man's "nature." This is precisely what the Book of Mormon is talking about when it discusses the nature of man, since it concentrates almost wholly upon the fallen nature of man's temporal existence and is not focused on his eternalism.[39]

If we go to the left side of the diagram and put a brace around our entire concept of man, it will extend from the top to the bottom of the whole vertical line; and if that brace includes the totality of Joseph's eternal ring, or what we often miscall the "eternal nature" of man, we absolutely must distinguish between the way we view our concept of man from the left side and the way we view it from the right side of the diagram. But a subtle clash of meanings lurks in the term "eternal nature" — it's oxymoronic, like "colorless paint" or "immaterial matter." The meanings of "eternal nature" are contradictory because the root of our word "nature" is *natus*, the Latin word for "birth;" and *natus* underlies *natura*, the Latin word for "nature," which refers to the internal, inherent, or inborn characteristics and properties of anything that is born or comes into the world. In talking about the "eternal nature" of anything, that is to say, we are talking simultaneously about something that neither begins nor ends on one hand but begins and ends on another.

This problem, at bottom, is irretrievably linguistic, since European words like "nature," *natura*, and *physis*[40] are inadequate for discussing the eternal aspect of the Latter-day Saint concept of man. It may be partially resolved by choosing the philosophical word "essence" to describe the left side of our diagram because, ever since the beginnings of philosophy in the sixth century B.C., "essence" has designated that permanent aspect of anything which is always or eternally present within it. Even that is not wholly adequate, however, because the revelatory and secular meanings of "eternal" obscure some rather subtle differences that are not always apparent. While participating in an academic seminar in the late sixties, for example, a Methodist friend and fellow classmate heard me say something about the fall of man and false ideas of merit that he had never heard from other Latter-day Saints; and in conversing with me about it after class, he asked me point-blank, "Do you believe that men are basically evil?" I could not speak, of course, for others in answering this query; but I had taught Book of Mormon classes at BYU for fifteen years by then, and my students had never tired of asking me essentially that same question. I had learned to answer it, moreover, by putting this diagram on the blackboard and pointing from the right side at "Nature," and from the left side at "Essence," and saying, "it all depends on the basis of 'basically' — if the basis of your question is mortality you answer it one way, and if it's eternity you answer it another way; so, which answer do you want?" That's where this diagram came from: it's my attempt to answer this very question for Book of Mormon students. The answer I gave my Methodist friend was therefore this: "I believe that all men are evil by nature; but I do not believe they are essentially evil." And his response to me was, "That's gobbledygook." Well, when we stop to think about it, that *is* gobbledygook if, in treating questions like this, we have assumed or presupposed the orthodox concept of man, which is the same from the left side of the diagram as from the right side. The answer I gave my Methodist classmate does not make any sense at all to anyone whose total concept of man begins with conception and has no place in it for premortal eternity. That, I think, is the nub of the whole problem, or very nearly so. I've learned to talk about the eternal essence of man — or whatever we choose to call it — because the Latter-day Saints, unless they are out of their minds, do not attribute universal evil to their total concept of man as an eternal being; but they *do* regard the temporal nature of man as universally fallen and attribute evil to it. We absolutely must make a clear distinction here, and the orthodox do not have to make it. And that, it seems to me, is an appropriate way to handle this.

All of which raises another thorny problem, as already suggested, for the Latter-day Saints. We have, in my opinion, an immensely complicated language problem; and in saying this, I do not mean that we should be using some language other than English (like German, French, or Italian): I'm saying that all of the Indo-European languages, and indeed all natural languages, are inadequate for discussing the eternal or supernatural essence of man.

## III. Brigham Young and the Natural Man

Now, what about Brigham Young? Where does he stand on this intricate and sensitive issue of the natural man? Typically enough, as with most issues, he eventually gets around to viewing this one from all sides; and his feelings about the natural man have often been misinterpreted, even by his followers. He is not perceived by many Latter-day Saints as a strong advocate for the doctrine of the natural man. Yet, he is precisely and exactly that. He runs head-on into the temporal language problem, of course, in discussing the eternalism of man; and some of the more broadminded Latter-day Saints are fond of citing volume 9, page 305, in the *Journal of Discourses* to show that he neither accepts nor advocates the doctrine of the natural man as taught by Paul in the New Testament.[41] It can be shown, however, if we understand where Brigham Young is coming from and where he's headed, that his famous disagreement with Paul is more a problem of language than anything else, and that he makes the words he uses mean what he intends them to mean because words are his *servants*, not his masters.

We can observe Brigham Young in relation to the temporal language problem in his remarks about Heber C. Kimball's use of words. "When brother Kimball speaks, . . . I easily understand his meaning; but he does not always fully explain his views to the understanding of the people. . . . Brother Kimball understands this doctrine as I do, but he has his method of expressing his ideas and I have mine; and I am extremely anxious to so convey my ideas to the people that they will understand them as I do." Brigham Young then makes this significant statement: "*Our language is deficient*, and I do not possess . . . the natural endowment that some men enjoy. I am a man of few words, and [I am] unlearned in the learning of this generation. The reason why brother Kimball has not language as perfectly and fully as some other men is not in consequence of a lack in his spirit, for he never has preached when I have heard him, that I did not know what he was about, if he knew himself. I know that his ideas are as clear as the sun that is now shining, and *I care not what the words are that he uses to express them.*"[42]

That suggests a couple of things. Words, on the one hand, mean absolutely nothing at all: they do not mean anything. But on the other hand, people *do* mean things by words, which acquire meaning only when they are given specific linguistic functions to perform. Brigham Young's remarks remind me of Humpty Dumpty, who, when Alice objected to his use of a word and complained that it didn't mean what he used it to mean, replied: "I can make a word mean anything I want, if I pay it enough!" That's the way Humpty Dumpty puts it; and in Bishop Berkeley's dialogue between Philonous and Hylas, Philonous says to Hylas: "I am not for imposing any sense on your words; you are at liberty to explain them as you please. Only, I beseech you, make me understand *something* by them."[43] Brigham Young does not care what the words are that Elder Kimball uses because he understands Elder Kimball: it is Elder Kimball, after all, who means whatever he means by means of the words he uses. President Young's only concern is that others may not understand Elder Kimball as he understands himself; and that, if there ever was one, is a language problem.

Brigham Young's comments about Heber C. Kimball were made on February 23, 1862; and six weeks later, on April 6, 1862, Brigham Young made another significant statement:

> No matter what our exercises may be before the Lord . . . , if our every day life does not accord with our profession, our religious exercises are all in vain. We may have all faith so as to remove mountains, . . . yet if we are not pure in our affections, true and fervent in our love for God, and holy in our spirits, all this will avail us but little. Our spirits should reign supreme in our bodies, to bring the flesh into subjection to the will and law of Christ, until the carnal, devilish spirit that fills the heart with anger, malice, wrath, strife, contention, bickering, fault-finding, bearing false witness, and with every evil that afflicts men, is entirely subdued. If this evil power is not vanquished by the power and love of God, the whole course of nature will be set on fire with the fire of hell, until the whole body and spirit are consumed.[44]

That's an interesting comment, coming as it does from a man who, in the minds of many, does not accept the Pauline doctrine, which is also a Book of Mormon doctrine, of the fallen, evil nature of man. Brigham Young continues, moreover, by quoting Paul as saying that "we are nothing without charity, whatever else we may possess," and makes still another significant statement:

> *Using my own language* I should say [that], without . . . the love of God in the heart to subdue, control, over-rule, and utterly consume every vestige of the consequences of the fall, the fire that is kindled within the nature of every person by the fall will consume the whole in an utter and irretrievable destruction. . . . In speaking of the tongue, the Apostle says, "But the tongue can no man tame, it is an unruly evil, full of deadly poison". . . . If this unruly member is not held in subjection it will work our ruin, for "The tongue is a fire, a world of iniquity, . . . it defileth the whole body, and setteth on fire the course of nature, and it is set on fire of hell." If the tongue is unbridled and uncontrolled, it sets in motion all the elements of the devilish disposition engendered in man through the fall.[45]

These comments about language are important, since they show very clearly that Brigham Young not only believes implicitly in the fallen nature of man but knows full well there is a language problem. "Our language is inadequate," he says, so he uses his own language and does not care what language Brother Kimball uses as long as both he and Brother Kimball *control* what they say and are not controlled by the language they use. He knows that he uses language in his own way, and that others do likewise. But he also knows that everyone must use the same temporal or time-bound languages in order to discuss *any* concept of man, including the Latter-day Saint concept of man; and that constitutes a problem when it comes to discussing the eternal aspect of anything. Brigham Young, like everybody else, must therefore use a temporal language in discussing our concept of man, whether he is speaking from the left side of the diagram about the eternal "essence" of man, or from the right side of the diagram about the temporal "nature" of man; and that makes him sound like he's contradicting himself when he really isn't. Brigham Young is in firm control of the words he uses, not the other way around; and our problem is to understand as clearly as possible what he intends the language he uses to imply. The Book of Mormon, furthermore, does not discuss the so-called "eternal nature," or what we have called the ultimate "essence," of man;[46] and that, too, is part of the temporal language problem.

Paul's statement about the natural man in 1 Corinthians 2:14 deserves close attention. Brigham Young made four or five comments about this statement that are very important, since his remarks about it in *Journal of Discourses*, 9:305, have often been quoted by those who do not like the scriptural doctrine of the natural man and cite this passage to prove that he didn't like it either.

> It is fully proved in all the revelations that God has ever given to mankind that they naturally love and admire righteousness, justice, and truth more than they do evil. It is, however, universally received . . . as a Scriptural doctrine that man is naturally opposed to God. This is not so. Paul says, in his Epistle to the Corinthians, "But the natural man receiveth not the things of God," but I say it is the unnatural "man that receiveth not the things of God" . . . . That which was, is, and will continue to endure is more natural than that which will pass away and be no more. The natural man is of God. We are the natural parents [of our children], and spiritually we are the natural children of the Father of light and natural heirs to his kingdom; and when we do an evil, we do it in opposition to the promptings of the Spirit of Truth that is within us. Man, the noblest work of God, was in his creation designed for an endless duration, for which the love of all good was incorporated in his nature. It was never designed that he should naturally do and love evil.[47]

We can understand something of the temporal language problem by looking at our diagram for the Latter-day Saint concept of man and remembering that, whenever we discuss either side of the diagram, we are "stuck" with the temporal vocabularies of time-bound *natur*-words in the natural languages of western Europe; and since eternal realities are of a markedly different order than temporal realities, our only recourse is to use the same *natur*-vocabularies in two different ways. In *Journal of Discourses*, 9:305, Brigham Young is clearly talking from the left side of the diagram about the eternal essence of man and saying we cannot label that as evil. He sounds here as if he is contradicting Paul; and yet, in other places, he doesn't contradict Paul at all. What he is saying, though, is very important and absolutely correct; but I would alert everybody to something Alan Cook used to say, "Beware of reading Brigham Young in paragraphs!"[48] We cannot simply isolate a paragraph from Brigham Young, read it carefully, and come away feeling that we know what he says about any subject: we must know most of what he says, and preferably *everything* he says, about a subject in order to understand how he felt about it. Alan would also say, if he were here, that there's more to it than reading excerpts from Brigham Young out of context, for there is something like a "principle of contextual insufficiency" that plagues us when we read him because he is a holistic thinker, and we cannot grasp the whole of his thinking about any subject matter unless we observe it in a sufficient *number* of contexts. Brigham Young is not an inconsistent thinker; but he does try to view virtually all subject matters from every side, and that makes him seem, especially to orthodox theologians and secular Mormons, as if he contradicts himself — which he rarely if ever does.

Three things should be pointed out concerning Brigham Young's comments on Paul's statement about the natural man. He said, first of all, that it was "the *unnatural* man," not the natural man, "that receiveth not the things of God." This is a dead give-away, since it clearly shows that, to Brigham Young in this particular context, the opposite of the "natural" man is neither the "carnal" man nor the "spiritual" man: it is specifically the "essential" man, or the eternal aspect of man that transcends nature in every way, which constitutes the opposite of the "unnatural" man in this comment by Brigham Young. This means, of course, that Brigham Young has redesigned the *natur*-vocabulary of his native English by replacing its temporal content with eternal content in order to use it for discussing the left side of our diagram. This becomes plainer still, secondly, when Brigham Young says, "That which was, is, and will continue to endure is more natural than that which will pass away and be no more." Here again, he is saying from the left side of the diagram that the eternal aspect of man, which we have called his "essence," is more "natural" than the temporal aspect of man, which the Book of Mormon calls his "nature." The real world, to Brigham Young, is therefore the eternal world, the world from which man came and to which he will return; and if we used the word "natural" as he uses it here, we could call the eternal world "the *real* natural world." It's "unnatural," Brigham Young is saying, to think about the eternal "essence" of man in the same way that Paul thinks about the temporal "nature" of man. That's why Brigham Young sounds as if he is contradicting Paul. But the truth is that both men are using the same vocabulary of *natur*-words in very different ways in order to discuss different aspects of the same thing; and that constitutes the whole sum and the entire substance of their infamous "disagreement"! Everything clears up when we realize that Brigham Young is using the same *natur*-words in two ways, depending on the aspect of man he is talking about — which is my third point: he does exactly that when he says that "the natural man is of God," that "we are the natural parents" of children in this world, and that "spiritually," or in relation to the world of spirits, "we are the natural children of the Father of light and natural heirs to his kingdom." Brigham Young is saying, in this context, that man is an eternal being who is just as "natural" in relation to the other world as our children are in relation to this world, and that parents, whichever world they inhabit, have "natural" children. Here, while discussing both the temporal and the eternal aspects of man in the same context, Brigham Young uses the selfsame *natur*-words in two very different senses; and our problem is thus to understand *him*, not to understand them.[49] He therefore concludes, in his celebrated comments of *Journal of Discourses*, 9:305, that whenever we do evil, "we do it in opposition to the promptings of the Spirit of Truth that is within us."

But why, if only the "unnatural" man is evil, do so many of us oppose this eternal spirit of truth so vigorously while in the flesh? The meaning of Brigham Young's answer to this question is now apparent without explanations. "Man . . . was in his creation designed for an endless duration, for which the love of all good was incorporated in his nature. It was never designed [by his Creator] that he should naturally do and love evil. . . . When our first parents fell from their paradisiacal state, [however,] they were brought in contact with influences and powers of evil that are unnatural and stand in opposition to an endless life. So far as mankind yield to these influences, they are so far removed from a natural to an unnatural state — from [a natural state of] life to [an unnatural state of] death."[50]

When Joseph Smith's eternal ring is severed, to sum everything up, we are brought into what Brigham Young calls "an unnatural state," a mortal state in which we die, whereas our "natural" condition is to live forever because we were created as eternal beings. Cutting Joseph's ring, accordingly, brings us into a fallen, mortal, sinful, and "unnatural" state of existence, since an endless life is "natural" to Brigham Young, and a life that ends in death is "unnatural" to him. That is clearly what he means by "natural" and "unnatural" in contexts like this; but we must remember Alan Cook's principle of contextual insufficiency, for we will not find Brigham Young talking like this in *all* contexts.

Paul's comments about the natural man in 1 Corinthians 2:14–15 are treated by Brigham Young in at least four additional contexts. The statement we have already examined was made on

June 15, 1862; but on August 3, 1862, only six weeks later, he made this statement: "The natural man (or as we now use the language, the fallen or sinful man) receiveth not the things of the Spirit of God: for they are foolishness unto him; neither can he know them, because they are spiritually discerned. But he that is spiritual judgeth all things, yet he himself is judged of no man."[51] Note the phrase "*as we now use the language.*" Brigham Young is fully aware that, in making the first statement we examined, he was using language in a different way than he is using it now because, whereas he was then discussing the eternal "essence" of man, he is now discussing his mortal existence. He is viewing the Latter-day Saint concept of man from the right side of our diagram, looking at what the Book of Mormon calls the temporal "nature" of man; and from this standpoint, or in his words "as we *now* use the language," the natural man is in very deed and actual fact "the fallen or sinful man." So, Paul is absolutely correct: the natural man, who constitutes "the fallen, or sinful man," does not receive "the things of the Spirit of God: for they are foolishness unto him; neither *can* he know them, because they are spiritually discerned." Brigham Young, who thus concurs wholeheartedly with Paul's doctrine of the natural man, now says: "In no other way can the things of God be understood. Men who are destitute of the influence of the Holy Ghost, or the Spirit of God, cannot understand the things of God; they may read them, but to them they are shrouded in darkness."[52]

We may wonder how Brigham Young can talk so differently, within only six weeks and almost in the same breath, about the nature of man. Our critics, both within and outside of the Church, often accuse us of being wishy-washy about this issue because they can't pin us down to take one side or the other of it. Well, if that's wishy-washy, then I guess we're wishy-washy; but we absolutely *must* make these distinctions in order to clarify where we are standing and which perspective we are taking when we discuss our concept of man. Our understanding of man is complex: we believe not merely in a dual but in a triune concept of the human being as consisting of an intelligence, a spirit body, and a natural body, all in one; and the orthodox concept of man is much simpler than this. That explains why Brigham Young agrees fully with Paul in both instances cited above and why assumptions based on the orthodox concept of man only make him *seem* to disagree with Paul in the first instance.

A second additional context in which Brigham Young mentions the natural man is dated January 10, 1869: "When we converse . . . on the religion we profess, we are apt to regard it as . . . unworthy . . . of the wise and to be passed [over] . . . by the great and noble. These reflections I have, and I presume others have them. Why is it so? The question can be readily answered by saying that the natural man is at enmity with God. That fallen nature [implicit] in every one is naturally opposed, inherently, through the fall, to God and to his kingdom, and wants nothing to do with them."[53] What could be clearer than that? It is as though Brigham Young, once again, were looking at our diagram from the right side, not from the left side; and once more, he is in perfect harmony with Paul. He continues: "Is there anything connected with our religion that is derogatory to . . . the most refined? No, there is not. . . . Is there anything in our religion that should startle the nations of the earth? No, there is not. . . . And yet we talk about it as though the people would be struck with wonder if we should tell them what it is. . . . We always talk and feel as though there is something or other about the Gospel of the Son of God that the people cannot bear. What is it?"[54] What they cannot bear is truth, according to Brigham Young, and especially *this* truth about the natural man, which the secular mentality, however sophisticated, has never been able to stomach.

The third additional context in which Brigham Young refers to Paul's comments about the natural man is dated July 24, 1870:

> God has commenced his Kingdom on the earth. How intricate it is, and how difficult for a man to understand if he be not enlightened by the Spirit of God! How can we understand it? . . . [We must] humble ourselves and get the Spirit of the Lord by being born of the water and of the Spirit. . . . How is it [to be understood] if we are not born of the Spirit? Can the natural man behold the things of God? He can not, for they are discerned spiritually — by the Spirit of the Almighty, and if we have not this Spirit within us we cannot understand the things of God. . . . What shall we do? Divest ourselves of great, big "Mr. I". . . . What next? [We must] humble ourselves before the Lord and receive the truth as He has revealed it, then we will be born of the Spirit. Then if we wish further blessings, [we must] be born of the water; then, if we wish further blessings, [we must] receive the laying on of hands for the reception of the Holy Ghost; and if we wish still further blessings, [we must] live by every word . . . spoken from the heavens.[55]

The fourth additional context from Brigham Young is dated April 28, 1872. He refers less directly, perhaps, to Paul's comments in 1 Cor. 2:12–14 in this context; but he does refer to them. "I am glad that I am not the Lord. And [I rejoice] to see the Latter-day Saints here [taking the sacrament and] following the example of the Savior . . . [who said:] 'Do this in remembrance of me until I come.' We are doing this to-day. Do not other Christians do the same? They do. How do we Latter-day Saints feel towards them? Were we to yield to the carnal passions of the natural man and we had the power of the Almighty we would spew our enemies out of our mouths, yes, we would hiss them from the face of human society for their evils, their malice, for the revenge and wrath they have towards us. But we are not the Almighty. I am glad of it."[56]

That, to me, is a moving passage; and before leaving it, let's go back to August 26, 1860, where Brigham Young, in a similar statement, repudiated the spirit of vengeance, the desire for revenge or what we might call the war spirit, that gets so many people fired up. That spirit had found place among the Latter-day Saints, and this is what he said about it:

> Some may think that they have passed through severe trials during the past few years; but . . . I have passed through no scenes of trial or sorrow. I have never felt better in my life than I have during two or three years past. I do not know that I have had wicked, unrighteous, or ungodly feelings . . . , though I may have felt desirous at times to lay righteousness to the line and judgment to the plummet, and sweep away the refuge of lies; but that would have only gratified that which pertains to the natural man. . . . It would not have satisfied that immortal part within us that is pure and holy, but partakes . . . of the weaknesses incident to the fallen portion. I have sometimes had feelings of this kind — "Draw your swords, ye Elders of Israel, and never sheathe them so long as you have an enemy upon the earth." I sometimes felt, before the move, like taking the sword and slaying my enemies, until they were wasted away. But the Lord did not design this, and we have remained in peace and quietness.[57]

The remainder of this paper presents selected statements by Brigham Young that do not refer directly to 1 Cor. 2:12–14 but are still about the natural man. The first statement is dated January 16, 1853:

> How difficult it is to teach the natural man, who comprehends nothing more than that which he sees with the natural eye! How hard it is for him to believe! How difficult would be the task to make the philosopher, who, for so many years, has argued himself into the belief that his spirit is no more after his body sleeps in the grave, believe that his intelligence came from

eternity, and is as eternal, in *its* nature, as the elements, or as the Gods. Such doctrine by him would be considered vanity and foolishness, it would be entirely beyond his comprehension. It is difficult, indeed, to remove an opinion or belief into which he has argued himself from the mind of the natural man. Talk to him about angels, heavens, God, immortality, and eternal lives, and it is like sounding brass, or a tinkling cymbal to his ears; it has no music to him; there is nothing in it that charms his senses, soothes his feelings, attracts his attention, or engages his affections, in the least; to him it is all vanity.[58]

The second random statement, dated December 18, 1853, pertains directly to but is not specifically about the natural man; but it pertains directly to the natural man, since it deals with the transition of every child of God, which begins with mortal conception and continues through natural birth, from an eternal to a temporal order of existence: "Many of you have fearful forebodings that all is not right in . . . this kingdom. You shiver and shake in your feelings, and tremble in your spirit; you cannot put your trust in God, in men, nor in yourself. This [fearfulness] arises from the power of evil that is so prevalent upon the face of the whole earth. It was given to you by your father and mother; it was mingled with your conception in the womb, and it has ripened in your flesh, in your blood, and in your bones, so that it has become riveted in your very nature."[59] The antecedent of "it," which occurs three times in the last sentence of this statement, is "the power of evil," which we inherit from our parents, they inherit from their parents, and so on—all the way back to our first parents. Conception is thus the mechanism of transition from man's eternal essence to his temporal nature, the means by which the fallen nature of our first parents is transmitted to their children, and to their children's children, etc.—all the way down to us. What we inherit from Adam and Eve, accordingly, is the temporal nature of their post-fallen condition, not the eternal essence of their pre-fallen condition. We do not therefore inherit any specific sins from them, for sinning is always personal and unique to individuals; but we do inherit from them the *ability* to sin, which Brigham Young calls "the power of evil," since, without the ability and the freedom to choose evil, there would be no agency and no possibility of redemption. The doctrine that children are conceived in sin nevertheless contradicts the secular beliefs of many people both within and outside of the Church. But it's definitely in our scriptures: it's clearly stated, for example, by

King David,[60] by the Lord himself,[61] and by Brigham Young, who understands clearly that only exalted Beings beget eternal spirits whereas fallen beings beget only temporal bodies. "The spirits of the human family are pure and holy at the time they enter tabernacles; but the Lord has so ordered that the enemy has great power over our tabernacles, whose organization pertains to the earth. Through this plan arises our probationary warfare. *Our tabernacles are conceived in sin, and sin conceives in them;* . . . our spirits are [therefore] striving to bring our bodies into subjection, and to overcome the Devil and the evils in the world."[62]

"This war and striving to overcome that evil power must continue until we triumph," adds Brigham Young, for "our spirits are [constantly] warring against the flesh, and the flesh against our spirits."[63] These struggles of eternal spirits with evils encountered through fallen temporal bodies are very real.

> *We have a [probationary] warfare.* . . . "We wrestle not against flesh and blood, but against principalities and against powers, against the rulers of the darkness of this world, against spiritual wickedness in high places." *This warfare commences within us.*
>
> The spirits that live in these tabernacles were as pure as the heavens, when they entered them. [But] they came to tabernacles that are contaminated, pertaining to the flesh, by the fall of man. The Psalmist says, "Behold, I was shapen in iniquity, and in sin did my mother conceive me." This Scripture has established in the minds of some the doctrine of total depravity. . . . This [doctrine] is not correct, yet *we [do] have a warfare within us.* We have to contend against [our own] evil passions, or the seeds of iniquity that are sown in the flesh through the fall.[64]

That, moreover, is not the end of it: "The pure spirits that occupy these tabernacles are operated upon" by *two* influences, according to Brigham Young; "and it is the right of Him that sent them into these tabernacles" to retain "the [ultimate] pre-eminence" among his offspring, "and to always give the Spirit of truth to influence the spirits of men, that it may triumph and reign predominantly in our tabernacles [as] the God and Lord of every motion."[65] "We not only have this warfare continually . . . within ourselves, but we also have an outside influence . . . to resist. Both the religious and the political world have [environmental] influences [for us] to contend against that very much resemble each other; they are more or less exercised, governed and controlled by surrounding influences. We Latter-day Saints [also] have an [external] influence of this kind to contend against."[66]

Brigham Young, finally, knows that evil exists in people and is realized in every human being and in all societies. "The evil that is spoken of," however, is *temporal,* not eternal, since it constitutes only "the power the Devil has gained upon this earth through the fall."[67] "He gained power to tempt the children of men, and wickedness is produced through their yielding to his temptations; but it is not [eternal] nature in them. *They are not 'conceived in sin and brought forth in iniquity' pertaining to their spirits: it is the flesh that is alluded to in that passage.* Then why not follow the [eternal] dictates of the Good Spirit? We talk about it, read of it, believe in it . . . [because] that Spirit which gives joy and peace to the children of men, and wishes and does no evil to any person . . . is the Spirit of the Gospel."[68]

The third random statement by Brigham Young, which is dated April 6, 1855, deals with defections from the restored gospel caused by naturalism: "Those who were not faithful, beholding things as the natural man beholds them, have left the Church: yes, scores of them, hundreds of them, thousands of them, both male and female. They looked at this kingdom, and, considering its progress upon seemingly natural principles, discovered it was best for them to leave it, and if possible save their lives."[69]

Brigham Young made the fourth random statement on June 7, 1857. He was referring to the fact that Latter-day Saints are unified by their belief in actual, live, ongoing, continuous revelation, and that this unity dissolves many things which tend to separate them. But their secular neighbors view that negatively and are angered by it. "There is but one fact that makes our enemies mad at us," he says, "and it is a principle visible and tangible to the natural senses, though I would not say that it is the internal workings of the natural senses to the natural man."[70]

The fifth random statement excerpts three paragraphs delivered by Brigham Young in the Bowery at Salt Lake City on July 19, 1857.

> When you look at things naturally, which is as far as the natural man sees, a person who takes a course to destroy himself temporally would be considered very unwise. And to the natural man we are taking [such] an unwise and unnatural course, wherein our religion is obnoxious to the Christian world. Did not your friends say to many of you, before you left your homes, that you were foolish — that the world would despise you and hate you? Did they not . . . say that you were very unwise . . . [and] that you had better stay where there was safety? They can see nothing more than

natural things; they do not understand the ways of God; they are unacquainted with His doings, with His kingdom, and with the principles of eternity.

So far as the natural man is concerned . . . the Latter-day Saints are very unwise to embrace in their faith those obnoxious principles that render them so odious in the eyes of the political and Christian world—the popular world. [But] the Latter-day Saints see further; they understand more than what pertains to this world. The Gospel of life and salvation reveals . . . that this world is only a place of temporary duration, existence, trials, &c. Its present fashion and uses are but for a few days, while we were created to exist eternally. The wicked can see no further than this world is concerned.

Can the wicked be brought forth to endure? No; they will be destroyed. . . . We all naturally know—we can naturally understand that man cannot stay here always. The inhabitants of the earth are continually coming and going. This is not our abiding place. All can see naturally . . . that this world is of but short duration to them. . . . It is but a short time, and then they must go.[71]

The sixth random statement by Brigham Young about the natural man is dated a week later on July 26, 1857: "What caused the men and women before me to leave their good farms, their good houses, their merchandize, and all the luxuries and comforts of life so dear to the natural man? . . . What caused all this? . . . Can any man tell? The world are trying to. . . . [But] they know not the reason why the people are assembled here; for they cannot and will not see and understand anything only as they discern it by the powers of the natural man."[72]

This paper concludes with an additional miscellany of random statements about the natural man by Brigham Young, which are presented without comment in order to get them on record.

*August 15, 1852: Two Excerpts.*—"The [knowledge] capacity of mankind . . . is great; all nations and people understand more or less of the knowledge pertaining to the arts and sciences. But when they leave those principles . . . comprehended . . . by the natural man, and undertake to define their own persons, their own being, . . . the propriety and wisdom of the creation, and bring forth . . . principles that pertain to future knowledge, . . . there is a veil over them. The veil . . . has beclouded their understandings, so that they are in thick darkness. This our experience teaches us—that when any uninspired person . . . [attempts to] step beyond organized nature, which is visible to the natural eyes, there is a mystery—the hidden mystery—the deep and unsearchable mystery of creation."[73]

"We can see the natural man, we can behold our face in the glass; but can we tell what manner of person we are? . . . It is a mystery to the wisest. . . . Philosophers are ready to acknowledge and exclaim, It is a mystery!—it is not to be fathomed or understood by man. When we advance into the future or recede into the past, either plunges a man into still greater mystery. It is a mystery that the world have sought after by their wisdom: they have studied diligently . . . , seeking to find that which others have not found—to learn that which has not been learned."[74]

*June 12, 1860.*—"The kingdoms of this world must become the kingdoms of our Lord and his Christ. To aid in accomplishing this work, we must overcome sin and every evil propensity of the natural man—every selfish and unhallowed desire. Let no man covet the things of this world, nor lust after the vain and foolish things that pertain to it."[75]

*September 30, 1860.*—"The heart of man is incapable of fully comprehending the blessings that God has in store for the faithful, unless he has revealed those blessings to them by the revelations of his Spirit. The natural man is contracted in his feelings, in his views, faith, and desires, and so are the Saints, unless they live their religion."[76]

*April 7, 1861.*—"Place ourselves back ten centuries, read the prophecies, and behold by prophetic vision what the Lord was going to do in the latter days. 'The time is coming when the Saints . . . will assemble themselves together. . . . Look forth in vision and behold these events.' They would appear far more beautiful than they appear to the natural man while acting in them."[77]

*March 6, 1862 (in dedicating the New Theater in Salt Lake).*—"Professing Christians generally would not consider this a fit position for those who profess the faith of the Lord Jesus Christ to occupy. [But] these Saints of the Most High appear here in the capacity of an assembly to exercise and amuse the mind of the natural man. This idea brings . . . a thousand reflections. What is nature? Everything that pertains to the heavens and the earth. 'My son,' says the Christian father, 'you should not attend a theatre, . . . nor a ball-room, for there the wicked assemble; you should not be found playing a ball, for the sinner does that.' Hundreds of like admonitions are thus given, and so we have been thus traditioned; but it is our privilege and our duty to scan all the works of man . . . , and thereby learn what man was made for, what he is capable of performing, and how far his wisdom can reach into the heavens, and to know the evil and the good [in man]."[78]

*March 23, 1862.*—"Many of us have been taught the doctrine of total depravity—that man is not naturally inclined to do [anything] good. I am satisfied that he is more inclined to do right [as an eternal being] than to do wrong [as a temporal being]. There is a greater power within him to shun evil and perform good, than to do the opposite. [But] we have the powers of darkness, or the influences opposite to good, to contend with. . . . There are two classes of influences, one tends to good and the other to evil; one to truth and life, the other to falsehood and death. Evil is sown in our nature, but there is not a person who is not prompted to do good and forsake evil; though there are but few who . . . will subject themselves to be perfectly obedient to the law of Christ, yet there are dispositions that will be subject to the truth through cruel mockings and scourgings, bonds and imprisonment."[79]

## IV. Addendum: Total Depravity
## and the Latter-day Saints

This last remark by Brigham Young about total depravity again presupposes the left-hand view of our diagram; but another aspect of depravity emerges if the right-hand view is taken. Latter-day Saints have traditionally rejected the orthodox language and vocabulary of depravity, not because they view the fall of man as somehow less than total, but because their total concept of man differs from the total concept of man in conventional Christianity. It is, after all, only a previously assumed concept of man that can be evaluated as good or bad — as nonfallen or as totally or partially fallen; and it must be acknowledged, as Mormon insists, that "in Christ there should come every good thing," since "all things which are good cometh of Christ," and that "otherwise men were fallen, and there could no good thing come unto them" (Moro. 7:22, 24). It must also be acknowledged, on the other hand, that the Greco-Roman optimism of Western rational thought has always been hostile to the radical insistence of revelatory pessimists that the natures of man and the universe are fallen. The intense anthropocentric *humanitas*, accordingly, which stems from the same Greco-Roman naturalism that civilized western Europe, has always repudiated the Christian doctrine of fallen man, whatever form it took, with its own antidoctrine of natural or inherent goodness. Since the natural order, on this account, is man's ultimate reality, it is the best thing he has to go by and his only means of evaluating anything; and since all who regard their ultimate realities — whatever they treasure most and give up last — as evil are insane, the natures of man and the universe are assumed to be good and contrary assumptions are not tolerated. But for all that, we must not be content with wrong answers to depravity based on humanistic objections to the fall of Adam, since they inevitably assume that man is good by nature whereas, according to our own latter-day revelations, the temporal nature of man, which deviates from the eternal essence of man, has indeed become depraved. Thus, the one and only instance of the word "depravity" in holy writ occurs in Mormon's tortured lament for the Nephites. "O the depravity of my people!" he exclaims. "They are without order and without mercy. . . . They have become strong in their perversion" — which is exactly what depravity means—"they are alike brutal, sparing none, neither old nor young; and they delight in everything save that which is good" (Moro. 9:18–19). Mormon's solitary use of "depravity," as a matter of fact, follows its basic meanings very closely, since they are derived from *de* ("from," "down from," "away from," etc.) and *prauitas* (any kind of "crookedness" or deviation from any kind of "straightness"), which combine to designate anything "twisted," "distorted," "perverted," or "contorted" by deviating from a standard that defines it as such. For all of our aversions to ortho-dox doctrines of depravity, accordingly, that word accurately describes the temporal nature of man, which deviates from the eternal essence of man because of the fall of man. From the very moment when Adam's pre-Cain children first "loved Satan more than God," therefore, "men began from that time forth to be carnal, sensual, and devilish" because of the fall; and their fallen state was shared by all men, since "all mankind," according to Alma, "were cut off from the presence of the Lord" and are "carnal, sensual, and devilish, *by nature*" (Moses 5:13; Alma 42:9–10; emphasis added)[80]—not spiritual, godly, and good by nature as the secular thinking of Greco-Roman naturalism would have it. This is the sticking point of our real dispute with total depravity as taught by orthodox Christians: they label their total concept of man as depraved; but we cannot do that with our total concept of man. Since people are either fallen or they are not and no one is partially (say 23 or 98 or 10 percent) fallen, we definitely affirm that everyone is totally fallen and is evil by nature; but we also affirm, since it is "because of the fall" that "our natures *have become* evil continually," that we are not *eternally* evil, and that "the natural man," who is in very deed "an enemy to God," has only been so "from the fall of Adam" and is not out of sync with God from all eternity to all eternity (see Ether 3:2 and Mosiah 3:19, where these implications of eternalism are definitely present; emphasis added). It is therefore our solemn duty and sacred privilege to proclaim the reality of man's total fall to everyone, and to offer relief from its negative consequences through the Atonement of Christ our Lord to anyone who loves redeeming light and truth enough to have faith in the Holy One of Israel, come to his Father's knee for mercy, and repent of all personal sinful-ness. We have nothing to offer anybody else.

# Notes

1. These are the six authors of the eight passages in the Book of Mormon that discuss the nature of man directly.

2. *Journal of Discourses,* 9:297. Still, he adds that "in the end . . . the living oracles of God have to take all things of heaven and earth . . . and prepare them to enter into the kingdom of heaven. Gold and silver, houses and lands, and everything possessed by the Saints will be purified . . . by the power of God . . . when the earth is sanctified." Emphasis added.

3. *Journal of Discourses,* 16:73–74, adding that "there may be some doctrines about which little is said in the Bible, but they are all couched therein, and I believe the doctrines because they are true, and I have taught them because they are calculated to save the children of men." Emphasis added.

4. Raymond Williams, *Keywords: A Vocabulary of Culture and Society* (London: Fontana, 1976), 184, adding (in ibid., 186) that "any full history of the uses of nature would be a history of a large part of human thought."

5. Peter Coates, *Nature: Western Attitudes Since Ancient Times* (Berkeley: University of California Press, 1998), 1.

6. Ibid., citing George D. Economou, *The Goddess Natura in Medieval Literature* (Cambridge, Mass.: Harvard University Press, 1972), 3, and 172, n. 5, who also adds that "Pauly-Wissowa devotes thirty-five columns to 'Physis,'" that "Arthur O. Lovejoy and George Boas list no fewer than sixty-six meanings of nature," and that "R. G. Collingwood has brilliantly traced and interpreted the views of nature from ancient to modern times" in his book, "*The Idea of Nature* (New York, 1960)." Consult also, in a truly voluminous literature about the idea of nature, many important studies such as C. J. Glacken, *Traces on the Rhodian Shore: Nature and Culture in Western Thought from Ancient Times to the End of the Eighteenth Century* (Berkeley: University of California Press, 1967), *passim,* and C. S. Lewis, *Studies in Words,* 2d ed. (Cambridge: Cambridge University Press, 1967), 24–74.

7. Translating *perfectus homo constat carne, anima, et spiritu* from Irenaeus Lugdunensis, *Adversus Haereses* 5.9.1. It is this three-way contrast between man's flesh (*caro*), his natural spirit (*anima* = the soul or animating principle of all natural life forms), and his revealed spirituality (*spiritus* = God's spirit and spirituality) that is so often overlooked today. *Perfectus homo,* which is properly translated as "the *perfected* man," refers, in this context, to the whole, complete, ideal, or total man. Thus, Irenaeus is discussing the just man "made perfect through Jesus" — through the Atonement of Christ and "the shedding of his own blood" — as "all the prophets . . . since the world began" have known full well (D&C 76:69; Mosiah 13:33); he is not referring to legally

observant humanists who try, however diligently, to perfect themselves through their own abilities to comply with ritual and moral requirements; he is stressing the very real difference between just men, who are made *vicariously* perfect by faith in the Atonement of Christ, and unjust men, who think they earn *personal* perfection through their own efforts without relying wholeheartedly on Christ and his Atonement.

8. Translating πάντες . . . εἰς ζωὴν ἀναστήσονται, ἴδια ἔχοντες <u>σώματα</u>, καὶ ἰδίας ἔχοντες <u>ψυχάς</u>, καὶ ἴδια <u>πνεύματα</u>, from Irenaeus Lugdenensis, *Adversus Haereses* 2.33.5. Emphasis added to stress Irenaeus' tripartition of elements in the early Christian concept of man.

9. Ibid.

10. Translating ὁ ἄνθρωπος συνέστηκεν ἐκ <u>σώματος</u> καὶ <u>ψυχῆς</u> καὶ <u>πνεύματος</u>, Origenes, *De Principiis* 4.2.4, emphasis added.

11. Translating ἐκ τριῶν εἶναι τὸν ἄνθρωπον . . . <u>πνεύματος</u> καὶ <u>ψυχῆς</u> καὶ <u>σώματος</u> from his fragment no. 88, emphasis added.

12. From ὡς ἐν τρισὶ τούτοις τὸν ἄνθρωπον ἔχειν τὴν σύστασιν . . . χάριν <u>τοῦ σώματος</u> καὶ <u>τῆς ψυχῆς</u> καὶ <u>τοῦ πνεύματος</u> from his commentary on Gen. 1:26.

13. Translating Οὗτοί εἰσιν οἱ ἀποδιορίζοντες, <u>ψυχικοί</u>, <u>πνεῦμα μὴ ἔχοντες</u> in Jude 1:19, emphasis added to distinguish the two spiritualities implicit in this sentence.

14. Paul's "natural man" in 1 Cor. 2:14 is the ψυχικὸς ἄνθρωπος, man as an immaterial ψυχή [psyche, natural soul, human spirit], not as a physical σῶμα [body] made of σάρξ [flesh].

15. The carnal man is the σάρκινος or σαρκικὸς ἄνθρωπος, the former meaning the "man who is made of flesh," the latter the "man who exhibits characteristics of the flesh."

16. Paul's "spiritual man" is the πνευματικὸς [ἄνθρωπος], which he contrasts with the "natural man" [ψυχικὸς ἄνθρωπος] in 1 Cor. 2:14–15.

17. Many of these sources are listed under ψυχή and its cognates in Henry George Liddell [et al.], *A Greek-English Lexicon* . . . (Oxford: Clarendon Press, 1989); Joseph Henry Thayer, *A Greek-English Lexicon of the New Testament* . . . (4th ed.; Edinburgh: T. & T. Clark, 1930); and William F. Arndt and F. Wilbur Gingrich, *A Greek-English Lexicon of the New Testament and Other Early Christian Literature* . . . (2d ed.; Chicago: University of Chicago Press, 1979). See also G. W. H. Lampe, ed., *A Patristic Greek Lexicon* (Oxford: Clarendon, 1961), 1542–54, which lists a multitude of pertinent sources and provides their original texts. And see, finally, W. K. C. Guthrie, *The Fifth-century Enlighten-*

*ment* ("A History of Greek Philosophy," v. 3; Cambridge: Cambridge University Press, 1969), 467–84 for an important discussion of the ψυχή as controller of the σῶμα in which the former is the soul—or natural spirit—of man that uses the latter as its instrument.

18. As in E. M. Blaiklock, "The Natural Man," *Greece and Rome*, 16, no. 47 (April, 1947): 52–53. This article not only identifies the natural man with the carnal man but fails to distinguish the spiritual man from the natural man in any meaningful way. Paul's term for "natural" is ψυχικός, which Blaiklock wrongly thinks "is almost equivalent to σάρκινος [made of flesh] or σαρκικός [having characteristics of flesh];" and to prove that, he cites three sources that refute it completely: *John Chrysostom*, for whom the natural man is ὁ μόνην τὴν ἔμφυτον καὶ ἀνθρωπίνην σύνεσιν ἔχων ["anyone possessing only inborn and humanly-originated intelligence"]; *John Calvin*, who defines the natural man as *quemlibet hominem solis naturae facultatibus praeditum* ["anyone endowed with only natural faculties"]; and *G. G. Findlay*, who says first that, "contrasted with the ἀκρατής [profligate], the ψυχικὸς [natural man] is the noblest of men," then that "to the πνευματικός [spiritual man] he is related as the natural [is related] to the supernatural," and finally that the natural man constitutes man's "unregenerate nature at its best." But—and Blaiklock sees no contradiction here—"Aristotle (*Eth. Nic.* III.x.2 [=1117.b.28]) used the word [for "natural"] to *distinguish* the pleasures of the soul [ἡδοναὶ ψυχικαί] ... from those of the body [ἡδοναὶ σωματικαί]." It is nevertheless incongruous to argue, following Aristotle, that "the ψυχικός had all the human excellence of the philosophers of Athens," since the immaterialism of Athenian form-philosophy rejected the Ionian physicalism of Democritean matter-philosophy implied in identifying the natural man with the carnal man. It is true, of course, that, "compared with the πνευματικός [spiritual man]" the natural man [ψυχικός] "lacks a whole dimension of his soul"; but the classical tradition knows nothing of a revealed component in its concept of man, and this insight is neither understood nor followed up. Blaiklock's insights, as a matter of fact, rest almost exclusively on the misidentification of natural with carnal realities; and it is difficult to imagine a more confused attempt to differentiate the natural man from the carnal man and the spiritual man.

19. For evidence see two of my articles, "The Central Problem of Intellectual History," and "Naturalism and Revealed Religion," in *Scholar and Educator*, 12, no. 1 (fall, 1988), 52–68, and 13, no. 1 (fall 1989), 17–31.

20. "*Saeculum*—a sequence of generations or even an infinite sequence of time—was related to [indefinitely long] ages of the world and to eternity," Philip P. Wiener, ed., *Dictionary of the History of Ideas* (New York: Charles Scribner's Sons, 1973), 3:477. Cf. Warren Wagar, ed., *The Secular Mind; Transformations of Faith in Modern Europe* (New York: Holmes & Meier, 1982), 234: "If one main branch of meanings ... [for] 'secular' derives from a Latin root which ... implied 'of or pertaining to the world,' there is a second branch whose sense is 'of or belonging to an age or long period.'" Thus, "to secularize

is to make secular, to bring into the *saeculum*, or 'world'. . . . This means to repugn or ignore religious considerations and substitute for them the values of 'this' world. . . . Secularization means the atrophy of belief in a . . . supernatural realm of being, and of institutions and practices grounded in such belief. . . . [It means] transferring the center of ultimate concern (to use Paul Tillich's phrase) from . . . supernature to the 'real' world of empirically observable nature, history, and man. . . . [It] is the process by which the supernatural has been lost," ibid., 2, 4–5.

21. Terms for the "carnal man," the "natural man," and the "spiritual man," unless otherwise indicated, will henceforth have the primitive meanings already attributed to them in this paper.

22. Transliterating ψυχή, the animating spirit of all natural life forms.

23. Transliterating Πνεῦμα, which normally refers to the transcendent spirit of God unless qualified by a contextual restrictor like an adjective, adverb, case form, etc. Its so-called opposite, ψυχή, means "pertaining to the soul or life" in the New Testament and related sources, "always denoting" as it does "the life of the natural world and whatever belongs to it, in contrast to the supernatural world, which is characterized by πνεῦμα," Arndt and Gingrich, 894.

24. From this point on, unless otherwise indicated, Greek words already cited in the footnotes will be italicized in the text and transliterated in conventional Augustan spellings that should be familiar to most English readers. New Greek words, if introduced beyond this point, will be handled the same way in the text and confined to their native spellings in the footnotes. Greek words "naturalized" by English usage will normally appear in quotation marks but may show up without them.

25. For ψυχικός and its adverbial form ψυχικῶς actually defined to mean "spiritual" and "spiritually" as opposed to "physical" and "physically" see Liddell, 2,027 and Lampe, 1,553–54. The same words, of course, which express only the secular spirituality of naturalism, can mean "unspiritual" and "unspiritually" from the revelatory perspective of Christianity.

26. Or *spiritalis homo* — both spellings will fly in Latin.

27. I have published this "full" or expanded translation of 1 Cor. 2:12–14, with only minor differences, in "A Sophic and a Mantic People," *BYU Studies* 31, no. 3 (summer 1991): 52. It rejects, of course, the word-for-word insanity of interlinear translation, but stays very close to the spirit and meaning of the Greek and Latin texts from which it comes. 1 Cor. 2:15–16, which I have not included in this translation, adds that people whose spirituality is revealed make judgments about all things, both natural and supernatural, without

being subjected to judgment themselves, because they possess the mind of Christ.

28. All direct references to the nature of man in the Book of Mormon are found in Ether 3:2; Enos 20; Mosiah 3:16–19, 16:1–5; and Alma 19:6, 26:21, 41:4, 11–12, 42:9–10.

29. Most direct references to the nature of man in the New Testament are found in 1 Cor. 2:12–14, 15:42–46; Eph. 2:3; 2 Peter 1:4, 2:12; and Jude 10, 18–19.

30. John Herman Randall, "Epilogue: the Nature of Naturalism," the concluding statement summarizing a monograph of fourteen critical chapters on naturalism in Yervant H. Krikorian, ed., *Naturalism and the Human Spirit* ("Columbia Studies in Philosophy," 8; New York: Columbia University Press, 1959), 354. Our English word "nature," Randall continues, "is the Latin version of the Greek φύσις," adding that "philosophic reflection arose in the Greek world when . . . thinkers in Asia Minor began to criticize their inherited beliefs by speculating on the φύσις or 'nature' of things. Greek wise men," he also adds, "early wrote books 'On Nature.' But what they were actually writing about had been a subject for debate ever since Aristotle . . . ; and it is [still] a theme for vigorous controversy among scholars," ibid. But the idea of nature, for all that, is a lot older than Aristotle.

31. Translating ἤμεθα τέκνα <u>φύσει</u> ὀργῆς ὡς καὶ οἱ λοιποί, emphasis added.

32. Those who regard the Book of Mormon as originating in early 19th-century New England, it seems to me, are at least tacitly acknowledging that they do not really believe it to be an ancient document, that it consists of something like inspired fiction invented by pious Americans for teaching religious principles, that it does not bind their consciences, that they can explain it fully in North America without referring to the European backgrounds of her earliest settlers, and that, in short, they do not take it seriously. But New England was not named for nothing, and the overwhelming majority of Americans, even today, are transplanted Europeans whose ancestors brought to their "new world" such geographical names as "New Orleans," "New Hampshire," "New Haven," "New York," and "Nova Scotia." Western European culture, accordingly, continues to dominate the civilizations of both American continents, although copious sprinklings of Athabascan, Asiatic, and other cultures are found among them.

33. This more or less summarizes Hugh Nibley's comments about "The Language of the Book of Mormon" in *The Collected Works of Hugh Nibley*, ed. John W. Welch et al. (Salt Lake City: Deseret Book, 1986), 896–97: "The original language of the Book of Mormon . . . seems to be stirring considerable interest in some quarters. . . . [But] such speculations are a waste of time. . . . Nephite was simply Nephite, as English is English, whatever its original

components may have been. . . . If we had the original text [of the Book of Mormon], which we do not, and if we could read it, which we cannot, any translation we might make of it would still be inferior to that which was given, as we claim it was, by the gift and power of God. . . . Scholars would be everlastingly squabbling about it and getting out endless new and revised translations, as in the case of the Bible. In fact, if our English text of the Book of Mormon came to us in any other way than by revelation it would be almost worthless! For members and investigators could ask of every verse: 'But how do we know it is translated correctly?' *A revealed text in English is infinitely to be preferred to an original [text] in a language that no one on earth could claim as his own.* . . . To the question 'What was the original language of the Book of Mormon?' the real answer is: It is English! For the English of the Book of Mormon comes by revelation, and no one can go beyond revelation in the search for ultimate sources."

34. Christ referred to the secular concept of eternalism when he said, "Heaven and earth" — the most eternal thing the secular mentality can think of — "shall pass away, but my words shall not pass away." Matthew 24:35; cf. Mark 13:31 and Luke 21:23.

35. Even the Lord himself, in revealing information about eternal realities unto those who have no recourse to eternal language, uses temporal languages, since "he speaketh unto men according to *their* language, unto their understanding" (2 Ne. 31:3; emphasis added). Thus, Moroni reports that Jesus "talked with me face to face, and . . . told me in plain humility, even as a man telleth another in mine own language" concerning the things of God (Ether 12:39); and Mormon confirms, conversely, that "there are many things which, according to our language, we are not *able* to write" (3 Ne. 5:18; emphasis added) because their language, like temporal languages generally, was not adequate for discussing eternal realities. This inadequacy of natural languages for communicating eternal information is also verified in D&C 1:24, 29:33, 90:11, and in Moses 6:5–6, 46, 57, 7:13.

36. Cf. *Teachings of the Prophet Joseph Smith*, comp. Joseph Fielding Smith (Salt Lake City: Deseret Book, 1938), 181: "That which has a beginning will surely have an end: take a ring, it is without beginning or end — cut it for a beginning place and at the same time you have an ending place."

37. See *Teachings of Joseph Smith*, ibid., 354: "I take my ring from my finger and liken it unto the mind of man . . . because it has no beginning. Suppose you cut it in two; then it has a beginning and an end; but join it again, and it continues one eternal round. So with the spirit of man."

38. Transliterating τέμνω, "cut."

39. Man's eternalism is everywhere assumed as true and taken for granted in the Book of Mormon, which is nevertheless silent, or very nearly so, about

such things as premortality, intelligences, eternal increase, temple work for the living and the dead, the eternity of matter, and many other aspects of man's everlasting coexistence with God in an infinite system of reality that has neither beginning nor end and lasts forever.

40. Transliterating φύσις, the Greek word for "nature."

41. A prime example of the above is George T. Boyd, "The Moral Nature of Man," an unpublished address to seminary and institute faculty at Brigham Young University, Provo, Utah, on June 29, 1962. Those who think this way also tend to reject the doctrine of the natural man as taught elsewhere in the scriptures by prophets like King Benjamin or the brother of Jared. I have personally heard an institute teacher in southern California, for example, teach openly in his classes that Benjamin was not a good Mormon because of his beliefs about the natural man!

42. *Journal of Discourses,* 9:286–87; emphasis added.

43. George Berkeley, *Three Dialogues Between Hylas and Philonous,* ed. Colin M. Turbayne (New York: Bobbs-Merrill, 1954), 40, emphasis added. Hylas means "materialist," of course, and Philonous means "idealist."

44. *Journal of Discourses,* 9:267–68.

45. Ibid.; emphasis added.

46. I keep saying "so-called" because I'm not satisfied with this term "eternal nature," and I'm still groping for a better term like "essence," or whatever we're going to call it.

47. *Journal of Discourses,* 9:305.

48. Alan Cook, now deceased, was formerly a professor of religious education and part-time instructor in philosophy at BYU.

49. Once we realize that Brigham Young uses the same language for discussing either aspect of man, but makes its words mean different things according to the aspect of man he is discussing, his contradictions simply evaporate—there aren't any.

50. *Journal of Discourses,* 9:305.

51. Ibid., 9:330.

52. Ibid.

53. *Journal of Discourses,* 12:323. Cf. Bruce R. McConkie, *A New Witness for the Articles of Faith* (Salt Lake City: Deseret Book, 1985), 282: "There is a natural

birth, and there is a spiritual birth. The natural birth is to die as pertaining to premortal life, to leave the heavenly realms where all spirits dwell . . . and to begin a new life . . . on earth. The natural birth creates a natural man, and the natural man is an enemy to God. In his fallen state he is carnal, sensual, and devilish by nature. Appetites and passions govern his life, and he is alive—acutely so—to all that is evil and wicked in the world. The spiritual birth comes after the natural birth. It is to die as pertaining to worldliness and carnality and to become a new creature by the power of the Spirit. It is to begin a new life . . . of righteousness, a spiritual life. Whereas we were in a deep abyss of darkness, now we are alive in Christ and . . . his everlasting light."

54. *Journal of Discourses*, 12:323-24.

55. Ibid., 13:271-72. Brigham Young once said, "Away with stereotyped Mormons"; and here he seems to be saying "Away with stereotyped sequences." It is not true that we are always born of the water first, and then we are born of the Spirit, and then we do this, and then we do that. These sequences are not unalterably fixed. In the Book of Mormon, for example, some of the Lamanites were born of the Spirit without even knowing what was happening to them; and here, Brigham Young says that, if we receive the truth as God reveals it, we are first born of the Spirit: then, if we wish further blessings, we will be born of the water, receive the laying on of hands, and so on. We have to do all of those things, but not necessarily in lockstep order.

56. Ibid., 15:2.

57. Ibid., 8:151.

58. Ibid., 1:2-3; emphasis added.

59. Ibid., 2:134.

60. "Behold, I was shapen in iniquity; and in sin did my mother conceive me," Psalms 51:5. Cf. Psalms 58:3, where David adds that "the wicked are estranged from the womb," and that "they go astray as soon as they be born, speaking lies."

61. "And the Lord spake unto Adam, saying: Inasmuch as thy children are conceived in sin, even so when they begin to grow up, sin conceiveth in their hearts, and they taste the bitter, that they may know to prize the good." Moses 6:55.

62. *Journal of Discourses*, 8:118; emphasis added.

63. Ibid., referring to Gal. 5:17 and adding that "to accomplish this, we must so yield obedience to the Divine influence as to learn the principles of eternal

life—to learn to bring the whole man—all the passions, sympathies, and feelings in subjection to the spirit. . . . All we have to do is to let the spirits that have come from . . . heaven reign triumphant, and bring into subjection everything that tends to evil: then we are Christ's."

64. *Journal of Discourses*, 10:105, citing Eph. 6:12; emphasis added. Brigham Young here characterizes total depravity as the false belief that fallen people are wholly bad and incapable of anything good, incapable even of choosing to accept or reject God's offer of redemption through the blood of Christ by faith, repentance, and rebirth because they are so sinful "that it is impossible for them to have one good thought, that there is no good, no soundness, and no spiritual health in them," ibid. For a near-perfect example of this false concept of total depravity, which is often thrown at Latter-day Saints by its protestant and other advocates, see Joseph Fielding Smith, *Selections from Answers to Gospel Questions* (Salt Lake City: Church of Jesus Christ of Latter-day Saints, 1972), 123–24, where President Smith rejects the bizarre sectarian insistence that parents, even if legally and lawfully married, must sin by having sexual relations in order to have children. President Smith's comments were evoked by a false but persistent interpretation of Psalms 51:5, the same passage discussed above by Brigham Young.

65. *Journal of Discourses*, 10:105.

66. Ibid.

67. Ibid, 7:190.

68. Ibid., 7:190–91. These same statements by Brigham Young also appear in *Journal of Discourses*, 6:330 where, in both accounts, he adds: "It is extensively taught that nature must be subdued, and grace made to take its place. I wish to inform you that it is [eternal] nature for the child to be influenced by the [eternal] Spirit of God. It is [eternal] nature for all people to be influenced by a good spirit." None of this negates, of course, Brigham Young's attitude toward the temporal nature of fallen man, which he regards as lost, fallen, and sinful.

69. Ibid., 2:248.

70. Ibid., 4:351.

71. Ibid., 5:53.

72. Ibid., 5:75.

73. Ibid., 6:284.

74. Ibid.

75. Ibid., 8:82.

76. Ibid., 8:188.

77. Ibid., 9:33.

78. Ibid., 9:242.

79. Ibid., 9:247.

80. This doctrine of man's fallen nature is consistently taught in all of the latter-day scriptures as well as in the Bible.

# Message Four

# The Constants of Conversion

*The doctrine that men and women must change, must be converted, is as old as the world. Adam and Eve were instructed by God himself that "inasmuch as ye were born into the world by water, and blood, and the spirit, which I have made, and so became of dust a living soul, even so ye must be born again into the kingdom of heaven, of water, and of the Spirit, and be cleansed by blood, even the blood of mine Only Begotten, that ye might be sanctified from all sin, and enjoy the words of eternal life in this world, and eternal life in the world to come, even immortal glory" (Moses 6:59).*

*As a living God, our Heavenly Father is forevermore involved in this matter of change. Because of the fall of our first parents and because men and women are often enticed to wander from the strait and narrow path, the Father sent his Only Begotten Son to alter the course of events on earth — to reverse what would otherwise continue as a movement toward spiritual dissolution. The Savior came into the world to change things, both cosmically and individually. The gospel of Jesus Christ is all about change, about the conversion of the human soul by and through the redeeming mercy and atoning blood of Jesus Christ. The world has its way of bringing about change, while the Lord and his prophets call for another way. The world focuses on rearranging, shifting, and effecting what prove to be cosmetic and rather temporary changes, while God calls for conversion, transformation, regeneration, and a lifelong change of nature.*

*The essay that follows deals with conversion, true conversion to Christ. In it Professor Curtis Wright focuses on some of the "constants of conversion," those elements associated with spiritual change that lead one from death to life, from darkness to light. This essay, like the others in this collection, is grounded in scripture, in the doctrine of Christ, and presupposes that recognition and conviction of sin are prerequisite to conversion and thus fundamentally necessary to salvation.*

*By now the reader has become well acquainted with Brother Wright's bold and straightforward discussion of the restored gospel. I find this essay to be thoughtful, provocative, and extremely beneficial to my own understanding of the process of conversion and feel confident that others will be likewise benefitted. It identifies within the New Testament and the Book of Mormon some of the central features of spiritual change so evident in the conversions of Paul and Alma. It demonstrates that conversion to Christ — rather than simply fascination with an idea, excitement about a new cause, or even a strong personal resolve — is what leads to permanent change (see Alma 23:6; 24:19; 27:27; 3 Ne. 28:23; 4 Ne. 1:2).*

*All men and women are called to come unto Christ and be perfected in him (see Moro. 10:32). Indeed, to choose to follow the Savior is to choose to be changed, "changed from [our] carnal and fallen state to a state of righteousness," thus becoming "new creatures" (Mosiah 27:25–26). This is Christian conversion, not a mere alteration in behavior patterns or even an acquisition of a few theological truths, but a deep-down change, conversion from the inside out.*

*Robert L. Millet*
*Dean of Religious Education, 1991–2000*
*Brigham Young University*

Is every authentic conversion to Christ unique, or is conversion to Christ the common experience of all authentic converts? Do different converts to the same gospel experience the same things? Or different things?

## I. The Conversion of Paul

Saul was converted to become the apostle Paul when the Lord convinced him of his sins.[1] Blinded by sudden envelopment in a brilliant, flashing light, Saul fell to the ground, where he saw the Lord, who spoke to him in Hebrew about his sinful past and told him of his future calling as a special "witness unto all men of what [he had] seen and heard," saying: "Rise, and stand upon thy feet: for I have appeared unto thee for this purpose, to make thee a minister and a witness both of these things which thou hast [already] seen, and of those things in the which I will [yet] appear unto thee" (Acts 22:15; 26:16).[2] So, Saul arose as Paul and was led by the hand to Damascus, where he fasted for three days before Ananias was sent to restore his sight, to prepare him for baptism, and to confirm that God had chosen him to "know his will," to "see his Just One,"[3] to "hear the voice of his mouth," and to "be his witness" in the great and wondrous work of redeeming both Jews and Gentiles (Acts 9:9; 22:12–16).

Paul, once converted and ever mindful of his sinful past, saw in his own conversion to Christ the prototype of all subsequent conversions worldwide. "This is a faithful saying, and worthy of all acceptation, that Christ Jesus came into the world to save sinners; of whom I am chief. Howbeit for this cause I obtained mercy, that in me first Jesus Christ might shew forth all long-suffering, for a pattern to them which should hereafter believe on him to life everlasting" (1 Tim. 1:15–16).

This saying emphasizes the basic elements of all conversions. Its message is πιστός and ἄξιος, according to Paul, which means "reliable" and "eminently worthwhile";[4] and its λόγος — its rational structure of intelligiblity — is unambiguous: "*the message that Christ Jesus came into the world to save sinners is trustworthy and must be accepted absolutely.*" That's what "worthy of all acceptation" means.[5] The redemptive purpose of Christ's atoning mission, his ceaseless labor of seeking and saving lost and fallen sinners, must therefore be taken seriously as the fundamental bedrock of revealed religion. When Paul says Christ saves sinners "of whom I am chief," moreover, the Greek word for "chief" is πρῶτος, meaning "first," by which he describes himself as the most sinful of all possible sinners — as the first and foremost number-one, triple-A, all-time champion sinner *par excellence*. But he felt this way only *after* being convinced of his sins by actual revelation; and that's how all authentic converts feel. They know, because God reveals it unto them, that their sins are not only real but dangerous, and they also know that the ultimate sacrifice of Christ's atoning blood, which was shed for them, is overwhelmingly paramount in their redemption and absolutely essential to their repentance and forgiveness. "I will work a marvelous work among the children of men," saith the Lord, "*unto the convincing of many of their sins,* that they may come unto repentance, and . . . unto the kingdom of my Father" (D&C 18:44; emphasis added). In order to redeem us, accordingly, the Lord himself must *convince* us of our sins, for we can neither repent nor come unto the Father without an authentic testimony — an actual revealed witness — of our own sinfulness, and it has ever been so. Forgiven sinners, like the Lamanites converted by Nephite missionaries, almost invariably think that prior to their conversions they "were the most lost of all mankind" (Alma 24:11). The Nephite missionaries themselves, furthermore, were convinced of their sins *before* they were converted: they include Alma the Younger, a malicious malcontent known far and wide as "a very wicked and an idolatrous man" whose father was president of the Nephite Church,[6] and four rebellious sons of King Mosiah, who once called them "the very vilest of sinners" (Mosiah 27:8, 28:4). This gang of five converted hoodlums, who became the finest and most capable missionaries in the Book of Mormon, have described in poignant terms what all converts feel when they are convinced of their sins by the Lord Jesus Christ. Thus, Alma the Younger, who was for "three days and three nights in the most bitter pain and anguish of soul" during his conversion (Alma 38:8), uses terms like "great fear and amazement," "racked with eternal torment," "harrowed up to the greatest degree," and "tormented with the pains of hell" in order to describe it (Alma 36:11–13); and Ammon, spokesman for Alma and the sons of Mosiah, describes the common experience of all five converts: "Who could have supposed that our God would have been so merciful as to have snatched us from our awful, sinful, and polluted state? . . . We went forth even in wrath, with mighty threatenings to destroy his church. Oh then, why did he not consign us to an awful destruction, yea, why did he not let the sword of his justice fall upon us, and doom us to eternal despair? Oh, my soul, almost as it were, fleeth at the thought. Behold, he did not exercise his justice upon us, but in his great mercy hath brought us over that everlasting gulf of death and misery, even to the salvation of our souls. And now . . . what natural man is there that knoweth these things? . . . There is none that knoweth these things, save it be the penitent" (Alma 26:17–21).

Paul, for all of his terrible sinning, resembles repentant sinners everywhere, who, whatever their unique and specific sins, feel the "crushing weight and killing curse"[7] of personal sinfulness as acutely as he did. On obtaining God's mercy through forgiveness of his sins, moreover, Paul's conversion became fully generalizable, thoroughly typical of real conversions wherever and whenever they occur, and it did this not only by revealing the full extent of the Lord's longsuffering toward notorious sinners like himself, but as "a formative pattern" discernible in "those who will yet have faith in Christ unto eternal life."[8] How, then, should we understand Paul's use of ὑποτύπωσις, which we have translated as "a formative pattern"? If we cannot go by the modern connotations of its appearance in English as "hypotyposis,"[9] we can at least point out that ὑποτύπωσις is an actional noun derived from the verb ὑποτυπόω, which refers to the constructive activity of forming, sketching, outlining, or characterizing the internal structure or inner nature of anything created from a common prototype — it is the imposed or "imprinted" residue of a predisposing pattern that will be found in *everything* created from that pattern.[10] If we understood "hypotyposis" as Paul understood it, we would interpret ὑπό as "foundational" or "fundamental" (like *sub* in "*sub*stantial," not like *sub* in "*sub*standard"), and we would also know that God's mercy to Paul, as to all who repent of their sins and come to him through Christ, was πρὸς ὑποτύπωσιν — for the sake of dismantling and reconstituting the natural framework of a fallen life[11] to accord with the basic or underlying constructive and patterning matrix, font, or mold that shapes, forms, structures, establishes, identifies, and authenticates the inner nature of every sinner it converts.[12]

Since Paul's conversion constitutes an authentic exemplar of the thing that creates all valid conversions, the formal structure of conversion is always the same, the same for everyone. But this sameness pertains only to the invisible patternment of conversion, not to its observable details. When a clothier, for example, manufactures hundreds of dresses from the same pattern, are the dresses alike or different? The answer, of course, is "Of course." The dresses are alike, if we speak conceptually of their production from a common prototype, since their intrinsic patterns are identical; but scientifically speaking, no dress is precisely and mathematically identical to any other dress, because dresses, even if made from the same pattern and cut from the same bolt of cloth, vary widely as to their observable components, which include such things as the materials, colors, weights, sizes, and accessories from which they are constructed.[13] That's the way it is with conversions. Their forms, their structures, their patterns are the same in every instance; but their experiential content is unique because everyone has unique experiences: we have ours, others have theirs, and nobody has anyone else's. We are "stuck," accordingly, with our own experiences, and we must live with that. We can discuss them with others, certainly, and they with us; but that's where it stops, for human experience is wholly personal, unique — and above all else — nontransferable. Nor can we experience anyone's conversion except our own because, while all conversions have the same spiritual forms, their empirical contents are inescapably unique.

## II. The Conversion of Joseph Smith

Since all conversions exemplify the same formal pattern, Paul's conversion, which was followed by long centuries of apostasy, anticipates and resembles in remarkable ways the conversion of Joseph Smith. The restoration of ancient gospel realities, which include every penitent sinner's conversion to Christ, has reinstituted eternal principles of revealed religion that do not change: they *cannot* change, for if it is eternally true that people are redeemed by the grace of God through faith in Christ, it was true for the ancients; and if it was true for them it is true for us:[14] we are wholly unredeemed, remaining in our natural state "as though there had been no redemption made,"[15] unless we are redeemed by grace through faith. Every conversion in holy writ, accordingly, conforms to the formal pattern of all other conversions, as does the conversion of Joseph Smith.

When organized in 1830, the restored church was commanded by revelation to keep a record of its history: that commandment was repeated in 1831 and 1832 (D&C 21:1; 47:1-4; 69:3-8; 85:1); and the first attempt to fulfill it is a six-page history prepared by Joseph Smith between the summer months of 1831 and the winter months of 1832, which contains our earliest account of his first vision.[16] This account, like our accounts of Paul's conversion, is a marvelous paradigm that exemplifies all of the basic elements found in the formal structure of any authentic conversion:

> At about the age of twelve years, my mind became seriously impressed with . . . all-important concerns for the welfare of my immortal soul. . . . Thus from the age of twelve years to fifteen I pondered many things in my heart concerning the situation of . . . mankind, the contentions and divisions, the wickedness and [the] abominations and the darkness which pervaded the

minds of mankind. My mind became exceedingly distressed, for I became convinced of my sins and ... I found that mankind did not come unto the Lord but ... had apostatized from the true and living faith. ... I felt to mourn for my own sins and for the sins of the world. ... And when I considered all these things, ... I cried unto the Lord for mercy, for there was none else to whom I could go and obtain mercy. And the Lord heard my cry in the wilderness. ... And he spake unto me saying, "Joseph, my son, thy sins are forgiven thee. ... Behold, I am the Lord of glory. I was crucified for the world that all those who believe on my name may have eternal life. Behold, the world lieth in sin at this time, and none doeth good, no not one. They have turned aside from the gospel and keep not my commandments. ... And mine anger is kindling against the inhabitants of the earth."[17]

That is a very significant statement, which should acquire even greater significance as it becomes more generally known, since it supplies essential elements that seem to be missing in other accounts of the First Vision; and it exemplifies the common source — the patterning, molding, shaping matrix — of all conversions, as do the conversions of Paul, Enos, Alma, or any authentic convert. Joseph, be it noted, does not speak empirically: he speaks in formal terms about the invisible mind of the inner man, not in physical terms about the corporeal brain or about the observable behavior of the outer man; and his concern is first for his own mind, then for the minds of others. "My mind," he says, "became seriously impressed with all-important concerns for the welfare of my immortal soul"; and those disquieting concerns for his own soul weighed heavily on his mind for three years; he took them very seriously, and we should do the same. We may not do it in the same way, but none of us can avoid the painful anguish of worrying, somewhere along the line, about our own souls.

Joseph also pondered, through the same three-year period, the situation of mankind. But unlike humanists, who evaluate man's situation optimistically in terms of his greatest and most marvelous accomplishments of art, architecture, literature, philosophy, and science, Joseph's view of mankind is pessimistic, since he evaluates man negatively by emphasizing the contentions, divisions, wickedness, abominations, and darkness that pervade the minds of all people. This somber mood, so discernible in Joseph Smith, does not suit the folksy humanism of latter-day morality: we elevate the positive, denigrate the negative, and deify cosmetic affirmations of human nicety that obscure our fallen natures and disguise the ugly face of reality. There's no doubt about it: when Joseph looked into his own mind and heart, and into the hearts and minds of mankind, he beheld the unveiled countenance of unredeemed corruption; and it wasn't pretty. But for all that, he didn't sober up or snap out of it or come to his senses. He went instead from being "seriously concerned" about human sinfulness to becoming "exceedingly distressed" by it. His were neither petty concerns nor minor distresses; and it was not his body but his mind — the thinking, sensing, and feeling part of him — that experienced them. These things had two important consequences. First of all, says Joseph Smith, "I became convinced of my sins:" that happened because he saw them clearly in his own heart and mind. Second, he adds, "I found that mankind did not come unto the Lord" but "had apostatized from the true and living faith"; and that occurred when he beheld the hearts and minds of mankind. This kind of talk, to be sure, seems strange and out-of-fashion today, especially among those Latter-day Saints who are oblivious to their own humanity: they don't like to hear about the sins of Joseph Smith because, like obsequious optimists everywhere, they believe in the power of positive thinking and want to see his good side.[18] But the Lord was converting the major prophet of this dispensation by bringing him face-to-face with the grim realities of sin within himself and in all others — in that specific order; and once convinced of sin within himself and others, says Joseph, "I felt to mourn" — in that same order — "for my own sins [first] and [then] for the sins of the world." These ways of mourning for human sinfulness, accordingly, come pretty much in sequence, since there's no use mourning for the sins of others if we don't mourn for our own sins. It was also thus with prophets in the Book of Mormon, who sorrowed for their own sins first, then for the sins of their people, and finally for the sins of the world.[19]

Joseph's reaction to these years of inner turmoil, finally, is instructive. "When I considered all these things," he says, "I cried unto the Lord for mercy, for there was none else to whom I could go and obtain mercy." And right there, at trail's end where human ingenuity failed him altogether, he found his way completely blocked: he couldn't go back, and there was no other path to take. All of us, furthermore, must come to this, for if any humanly originated way out of our fallen predicament remains open to us, we will take it: we must therefore know by one form of revelation or another, even as Jacob knew and delighted in proving to his people, "that save Christ should come all men must perish"; for as Amulek also knew by revelation, "there must be an atonement made, or else all mankind must unavoidably perish" because "all are hardened; yea, all are fallen and are lost, and must perish except it be through the atonement which it is expedient should be made" (2 Ne. 11:6; Alma 34:9). It's only when the Lord himself convinces us of our sins[20] — when we realize fully and understand without ambiguity "that there is no other way nor means whereby man can be saved" *except* "through the atoning blood of Jesus Christ" (Hel. 5:9),[21] and when we finally come to see (not through a glass darkly but face-to-face with our sins and very clearly) that every other avenue to peace with God is closed — that we, like Joseph Smith, will turn to the Lord and plead with him for mercy because there is no one else to help us and nowhere else to go. Thus, in following the pattern implicit in all conversions, Joseph tells us, "the Lord heard my cry in the wilderness"; and "he spake unto me, saying, 'Joseph, my son, thy sins are forgiven thee'" — which means, if the six-page history of 1831–32 is the earliest and truest account of the First Vision, that this statement was the first message revealed by the Lord to Joseph Smith. In what he said very plainly after forgiving Joseph's sins, moreover, the Lord also emphasized the redeeming nature and absolute necessity of his atoning mission among the children of men through his Father's restoration of the gospel. This he did in two ways: (1) he spoke about his own work of salvation — about his divine life and redeeming mission among his Father's children; and (2) he explained the estrangement of all mankind from his Father's world by their presence in another world — a lost and fallen world that separated them from their heavenly parents and exposed them to all kinds of evil influences. Those were the burning issues in the mind of Joseph Smith for three years running. But then, at long last, he heard the Savior say: "Behold, I am the Lord of Glory. I was crucified for the world that all those who believe on my name may have eternal life." This constitutes an extraordinary verification of Paul's faithful saying "that Christ Jesus came into the world to save sinners": the Lord is saying the same thing here. And finally, referring to the lost and fallen predicament of all mankind, the Lord said to Joseph in plain language: "Behold, the world lieth in sin at this time, and none doeth good, no not one. They have turned aside from the gospel and keep not my commandments. . . . And mine anger is kindling against the inhabitants of the earth." These are the fundamental principles of all gospel thinking, the foundational doctrines of the fall of man and the Atonement of Christ, which were revealed to Joseph Smith only after he turned to the Lord and cried unto him for mercy. They are indispensable to revealed religion, since they constitute the most basic of all elements in the formative pattern-ment of conversion that is so prominent in the thinking of every authentic convert.

## III. The Conversion of Enos

Not all Latter-day Saints read the Book of Mormon carefully; but the thing that comes most readily to mind in its careful readers, once they see the same pattern of formal constants in the conversions of Paul and Joseph Smith, is probably the conversion of Enos. He was first and last a keeper and recorder of the Nephite scriptures, for we meet him first when he accepts responsibility for the sacred record from his father (Jacob 7:27) and last when he confers it on his son (Jarom 1:1–2). This pattern of conversion, which is eminently discernible in the conversion of Enos, holds great meaning for many Latter-day Saints: they weep real tears over it; and more of us, perhaps, should be moved to tears by its overwhelming presence in Joseph's account of his own conversion.

The gospel didn't register with Enos at first, although he speaks of his father as a man of faith who consistently taught it to him. He, too, had to be converted, and therefore he says, "I will tell you of the wrestle which I had before God, before I received a remission of my sins" (Enos 1:2). His use of the word "wrestle" seems intentionally unsettling: it implies the trauma, confusion, uncertainty, futility, and unrelieved combativeness of prolonged struggling to withstand powerful assailants and to understand his own precarious existence in a dangerous world that made little sense to him. But that's how Enos tells his story of wrestling before God with the terrible spirits of unbelief. "Behold," he says, "I went to hunt beasts in the forests; and the words which I had often heard my father speak concerning eternal life, and the joy of the Saints, sunk deep into my heart" (Enos 1:3). Enos thus foreshadows the conversion of Alma, who would also remember, while in the throes of conversion, that he had often heard his father speak of those same things without knowing what they meant until, in the depths of anguished sorrow for his sins, they finally penetrated his consciousness. So one day, while hunting for game in a forest,[22] Enos was overwhelmed with memories of his father's great concern for the words of eternal life and the joy of the Saints. His mind, accordingly, was flooded with these things, which found their way into his heart by seeping into his very being. "And my soul hungered," says Enos, since these were not temporal problems to be resolved by scholarly research if studied critically in reformed Egyptian: they were eternal problems that God resolves only for those who hunger and thirst after righteousness. It was not the body, furthermore, but the *soul* of Jacob's son that needed nourishment. Therefore, Enos continues, "I kneeled down before my Maker, and I cried unto him in mighty prayer and supplication for mine own soul; and all the day long did I cry unto him; yea, and when the night came I did still raise my voice high that it reached the heavens" (Enos 1:4). This is the "mighty prayer" passage that's so important in the Book of Mormon—the passage in which Enos prays mightily all day long and well into the night for his own soul. This has to be one of the most earnest, sincere, and mighty prayers ever uttered, for few of us can kneel hypocritically and pray insincerely for fifteen minutes without falling to sleep on our knees; but Enos wrestled before God in earnest prayer for something like fifteen hours of genuine concern for the welfare of his eternal soul. What could that be if not mighty prayer? Surely that implies massive concern, great distress, and much anguish of soul over long periods of time.

Enos really went through it, apparently, for conversion didn't come easily to him; but after all that, he tells us, "there came a voice unto me, saying: Enos, thy sins are forgiven thee, and thou shalt be blessed" (Enos 1:5).[23] Must everyone, then, hear a voice in order to be converted and forgiven of their sins? Paul, Alma, Enos, and Joseph Smith certainly did; but here again, the answer is "No." Sinners don't always see visions or hear voices when they are converted. What *does* have to occur in every conversion, however, is actual communication from God in the other world to someone in this world; and diordinal communication of this kind is strictly vertical: it always comes from the top down, from a higher to a lower order of being, because it constitutes supernatural contact that is very real, cannot be controlled or manipulated by natural beings or processes, and can only be revealed. This contact must be initiated by God himself and implemented personally or through one of his agents—his Beloved Son, the Holy Ghost, an angel, someone you know (like a bishop, teacher, wife, parent, husband, child, neighbor, or friend), or even a stranger—but actual contact has to be made, and it must be real. It cannot be reduced to patriotic fervor or zeal for cultural religion, since the whole purpose of the gospel is to bring individuals in our world into actual contact with the redeeming power of God's world. Once contact is established, furthermore, the individual contacted must respond to it positively or negatively, for that response is personal and cannot be delegated. Our secretaries can't decide what we should do with it: only we can decide that; but contact must be made; and this means that, when sinners like Enos or Joseph Smith repent of their sins through faith in Christ, they must know, because God reveals it to them, that he accepts their faith and repentance and forgives their sins. This kind of knowledge, which is not humanly originated like natural knowledge, must be revealed from a source higher than human beings because, since God alone can forgive sins, penitent sinners have no way of knowing their sins are forgiven *except* by revelation. Revealed knowledge, accordingly, constitutes the most essential component of conversion; and the actual communication of revealed knowledge, which must be communicated by God to man or remain uncommunicated, thus lies at the very heart of all authentic conversions: it is our only means of access to "the peace of God, which passeth all understanding" (Phil. 4:7) and brings the emancipating joy of knowing by his own revealed witness unto us that God accepts our faith and repentance and forgives our sins.

How important is it, really, to know by revelation that our sins are forgiven? We should know this, to be sure; and according to the Sixth Lecture on Faith, it should not be a matter of guesswork or uncertainty. Nor can this be learned by studying books or taking courses of instruction from professors: it can come *through* such things, of course, but it never comes *from* them. It comes any way God wants it to come. And that's the whole point. Knowledge revealed by God does not come from God's ways of communicating information: it comes from God; and it doesn't always come in the same way. But—and this is crucially important—*peace does come to converts.* "I, Enos," to cite one of them, "knew that God could not lie; wherefore, my guilt was swept away" (Enos 1:6). Once he knows that God forgives his sins, in other words, his guilt vanishes: it's gone. And Enos can only ask in amazement: "Lord, how is it done?" That it could be done at all was to him, as it is to every convert, a marvelous and mysterious thing. Miracles are seemingly scarce and getting scarcer in our world; but valid conversions that are actually experienced and authentically real are probably the greatest miracles of all. Can anyone possibly imagine anything more miraculous in a lost and fallen world than secular people who somehow get their heads on straight about revealed religion? Well, converts do just that. It happens every day; and every convert, like Enos marveling at his own conversion, asks, "Lord, how is it done?" The answer, as it was to Enos, is: "Because of thy faith in Christ, whom thou hast never before heard" — meaning *really listened to* — "nor seen. . . . Wherefore, go to, thy faith hath made thee whole" (Enos 1:7-8). Sinners are not converted because they are latent geniuses with lofty ideals, or because they pursue worthwhile goals, or because they know the right people and have powerful friends in high places, or because they desire wealth and earn it honestly through skilful planning and productive work, or because they merit the praise of the world in any way at all: conversions occur only when repenting sinners obtain God's forgiveness through redeeming faith in the atoning blood of Jesus Christ; and where redeeming faith in Christ is not, there are no conversions whatever, not a single one.

That was the faith of Enos, the faith that makes forgiven sinners whole. It's not the clinically ill alone who need wholeness, accordingly, for like Enos, sinners can be spiritually sick in perfect health: it's only when their faith and repentance are accepted and God forgives their sins that they are made whole; and all of that follows from faith. Sequencing is therefore significant in the conversion of Enos, whose concern was *first* for his own soul, as in Joseph Smith, and *then* for the souls of others. His second concern was thus for the Nephites, and his third for the Lamanites. Once forgiven, says Enos, "I began to feel a desire for the welfare of my brethren, the Nephites; wherefore, I did pour out my whole soul unto God for them. And while I was thus struggling in the spirit, behold, the voice of the Lord came into my mind again, saying: I will visit thy brethren according to their diligence in keeping my commandments. . . . And their transgressions will I bring down with sorrow upon their own heads" (Enos 1:9–10). That wasn't exactly what Enos wanted to hear: the Lord didn't say everything would work together for good unto the Nephites or all would be well with them. Their future, Enos knew, was not entirely rosy; but he also knew, since the Lord had dealt mercifully with him, that the Lord would deal mercifully with them; and as it once was with the Nephites it still is with the Latter-day Saints, for God forgives and converts those among them who have faith in Christ and repent of their sins, just as he forgave and converted Enos and Joseph Smith.

Enos, finally, was filled with compassion for his Lamanite brethren, as his faith "began to be unshaken in the Lord" (Enos 1:11). That leaves most of us wondering what unshakable faith is like, for our faith can indeed be shaken. Still, insofar as we live by actual faith and a genuine hope in Christ, we approach the unshakable faith of Enos, who prayed unto the Lord "with many long strugglings for . . . the Lamanites" (Enos 1:11). His heart's desire was that God would preserve the record of his people, the Nephites, and bring it unto his estranged brethren, the Lamanites.[24] Enos was wary of the Nephites and their future; but his great desire, if they should fall into sin and be destroyed, was that their record might one day find its way to the Lamanites. He lived in a day, he says, when "our strugglings were vain in restoring them to the true faith. And they swore in their wrath that . . . they would destroy our records and us, and also all the traditions of our fathers" (Enos 1:14). Thus, Nephites and Lamanites killed each other on sight in his day; and although the Nephites "did seek diligently to restore the Lamanites unto the true faith in God," he tells us, "our labors were vain" because "their hatred was fixed, and they were led by their evil nature that they became wild, and ferocious, and a bloodthirsty people, full of idolatry and filthiness; . . . and they were continually seeking to destroy us" (Enos 1:20).[25] "Wherefore, . . . knowing that the Lord God was able to preserve our records, I cried unto him continually, for he had said unto me: Whatsoever thing ye shall ask in faith, believing that ye shall receive in the name of Christ, ye shall receive it. And I had faith, and I did cry unto God that he would preserve the records; and he covenanted with me that he would bring them forth unto the Lamanites in his own due time. And I, Enos, knew it would be according to the covenant which he had made; wherefore my soul did rest. And the Lord said unto me: Thy fathers have also required of me this thing; and it shall be done unto them according to their faith; for their faith was like unto thine" (Enos 1:15–18).[26]

Enos speaks, lastly, of apostasy among the Nephites, and of his own prophetic ministry. "There were exceedingly many prophets among us," he says, for "the [Nephite] people were a stiffnecked people, hard to understand" (Enos 1:22). This doesn't mean it was hard for the prophets to understand the Nephites: it means it was hard for the Nephites to understand the gospel; and if that verse is instructive, the next one is amazing: "There was nothing save it was exceeding harshness, preaching and prophesying of wars, and contentions, and destructions, and continually reminding them of death, and the duration of eternity, and the judgments and the power of God, and all these things — stirring them up continually to keep them in the fear of the Lord. I say there was nothing short of these things, and exceedingly great plainness of speech, would keep them from going down speedily to destruction" (Enos 1:23).

That's a marvelous portrait of an unstable civilization by a citizen-prophet who saw only wars between Nephites and Lamanites in the course of his days (Enos 1:24). So, he bids farewell; and in spite of everything, because he had been authentically converted and remained true to his calling, things had gone well with him, if not for his people. "I must," he says, "soon go down to my grave, having been wrought upon by the power of God that I must preach and prophesy unto this people, and declare the word according to the truth which is in Christ. . . . I have declared it in all my days, and have rejoiced in it above that of the world. And I soon go to the place of my rest, which is with my Redeemer; for I know that in him I shall rest. And I rejoice in the day when my mortal shall put on immortality, and shall stand before him; then shall I see his face with pleasure, and he will say unto me: Come unto me, ye blessed, there is a place prepared for you in the mansions of my Father" (Enos 1:26–27).

Enos was thus a penitent sinner who was converted when he was "wrought upon by the power of God." He *knew*, by actual revelation while in this life, that his repentance and faith in Christ were accepted by God, that his sins were forgiven by God, that he rejoiced in the word of God above all else, that he was called by

God to teach "the truth which is in Christ" all his days, that he could stand before God in judgment without shame or fear of punishment, and that God had reserved a place for him on high. Here's a man who actually rejoiced in the thought of coming into the presence of God to be judged of his deeds – it thrilled him to think of it! Few, indeed, are delighted when they think of coming to the bar for judgment. Alma, for example, was panicked at the thought – *until* he was converted. But that's Enos. His is perhaps the foremost story in the Book of Mormon suggested by our earliest account of Joseph Smith's conversion.

## IV. The Conversion of Alma

Alma exemplifies the urgent necessity of bringing those who are headed for destruction unto repentance by convincing them of their sins. He was caught up, less than two decades after Benjamin's death, in a powerful anti-Christ movement among the Nephites. This movement, like the attempt of the French Revolution to dechristianize Europe,[27] constituted an all-out cultural revolt of unbelievers against believers, pitted "the rising generation" of young intellectual radicals against the traditions of their fathers, and institutionalized the permanent sophic–mantic divisiveness that eventually destroyed Nephite civilization (Mosiah 26:1–5). Youthful revolutionaries like Alma and the sons of Mosiah, accordingly, were not only sinners but *criminals*, since their actions were meant to dethrone "God, or even the king" (Mosiah 27:10).[28]

Alma tells the sordid story of his anti-Christian radicalism to his sons and explains his subsequent conversion to Christ.[29] "I do know," he says, that those who "put their trust in God shall be supported in their . . . afflictions, and . . . lifted up at the last day"; and since these things can be known only by revelation, he adds, no one should "think that I know of myself," since his knowledge is "not of the temporal but of the spiritual, not of the carnal mind but of God" (Alma 36:3–4). That clarifies the nature and the source of Alma's knowledge, which was neither humanly originated nor humanly communicated. His was revealed – not speculative – knowledge. He didn't get it from men: he got it from the Father, who teaches "everyone that hearkeneth to . . . the Spirit" of his Son about the new and everlasting covenant of redemption, "which he has renewed and confirmed" in our day "for the sake of the whole world" (D&C 84:47-48). This presupposes an ineluctable difference between natural knowledge, which everyone of normal sensory and intellectual ability possesses, and revealed knowledge, which everyone born of God possesses. Thus, Alma tells his sons, "if I had not been born of God I should not have known these things; but God has, by the mouth of his holy angel, made these things known unto me, not of any worthiness of myself"; for "never, until I did cry out unto the Lord Jesus Christ for mercy, did I receive a remission of my sins" (Alma 36:5, 38:8).[30] Alma, certainly, did not "earn" revealed knowledge of his forgiveness through personal worthiness: he came to see exactly what he deserved from God when confronted by an angel—and didn't want to get it; he confessed his unworthiness freely before God and before all men after that; and he counseled others to do likewise.[31] "I went about with the sons of Mosiah," he recalls, "seeking to destroy the church of God." That was his acknowledged goal; and by his own admission he pursued it relentlessly until "God sent his holy angel to stop us by the way" (Alma 36:6).

Then follows an account of the angel's sudden appearance, his terrible voice of thunder that shook the earth where Alma stood with his friends and made it tremble beneath their feet, and the dreadful fear of the Lord that enveloped all who heard it and threw them to the ground (Alma 36:7-8). That awful voice, Alma tells us, then "said unto me: Arise. And I arose. . . . And he said unto me: If thou wilt of thyself be destroyed, seek no more to destroy the church of God" (Alma 36:9). This thunderous utterance conceals a Semitic idiom that makes it difficult for us to understand;[32] but Alma understood it perfectly, as though the angel had said to him: "If you want to be destroyed, you miserable wretch of a man,[33] just keep on doing what you're doing and it will happen; so take this warning to heart: let it sink down into your ears, lest your destruction be made sure, and seek no more to destroy the church of God!"[34] On hearing that, Alma tells us, he fell again to the earth, where he was motionless for three days and three nights. "I could not open my mouth," he says, "neither had I the use of my limbs" (Alma 36:10). He was accordingly insensate and comatose, dead to the world he lived in, although he still had a pulse (if anyone had known how to take it) and his forehead wasn't cold; but he was going through abject misery in the world that lived in him. "The angel spake more things unto me," he recalls, "but I did not hear them; for when I heard the words — If thou wilt be destroyed of thyself, seek no more to destroy the church of God — I was struck with such great fear and amazement lest perhaps I should be destroyed, that I fell [again] to the earth and I did hear no more" (Alma 36:11). Before that, apparently, and like most young men, he had never given a thought to temporal death, to say nothing of eternal destruction. But now, and all at once, he had to face the very real possibility of actually being destroyed; and that finally got to him. "I was racked with eternal torment," he tells us, "for my soul was harrowed up to the greatest degree and racked with all my sins. Yea, I did remember all my sins and iniquities, for which I was tormented with the pains of hell" (Alma 36:12–13). An amazing statement, that, for ere long he'll say he's *forgotten* all his sins; but for now, he says, "I saw that I had rebelled against my God, and that I had not kept his holy commandments" (Alma 36:13). Alma therefore went through the agonizing reorientation experienced by all authentic converts that finally convinced him of his sins. Before conversion, apparently, it never occurred to him that he was sinful. This he had to discover by being converted himself: he had to go through the brutalizing process of rethinking *everything* in order to see clearly that he was rebelling against God and breaking his commandments. And though we can easily talk ourselves out of it, all of us must come to this. "I'm not as bad as the scriptures say," we tell ourselves and others, or "Look at my neighbors: they're *much* worse than I am!" It's duck soup to talk it all away. Humanists and intellectuals, for example, tell us constantly that there's nothing to forgive, since there's no such thing as sin and no one to forgive it, so just pass it off and forget it and it'll go away. But Alma, who once thought that way, could think that way no more: he even says that he had murdered many of God's children, although he wasn't referring to murder one. Still, he had come to believe that leading people away unto destruction was a kind of spiritual murder that was very like, and almost as bad as, first-degree murder. "And in fine," he concludes, "so great had been my iniquities that the very thought of coming into the presence of my God did rack my soul with inexpressible horror. Oh, thought I, that I could be banished and become extinct both soul and body, that I might not be brought to stand in the presence of my God, to be judged of my deeds" (Alma 36:14–15). That's how much Alma came to fear the judgments of God: he actually preferred the nonbeing of annihilation — going out of existence altogether and utterly ceasing to be in any way, at any time, or anywhere at all — to being in the presence of God; and that's how it went with him for three days and three nights. His conversion, however described, was a wrenching, wretched, and wresting experience: his pains were real, sustained, and excruciatingly severe; and his mind, to use Joseph Smith's term, was extensively and "exceedingly distressed." But at long last, while deeply enmeshed in writhing convulsions of repentance, Alma thought of something else — something far greater than the memory of his many sins and their awful consequences: "I remembered also," he says, "to have heard my father prophesy unto the people concerning the coming of one Jesus Christ, a Son of God, to atone for the sins of the world" (Alma 36:17). That had never meant anything to him before: he had heard a lot about it, to be sure, from Alma the Elder; but now, while in such pain and so much distress for his sinfulness, the realization that Christ was coming into the world to atone for sins like his took hold of him, acquired great and unmistakable meaning, and would not let go. Nor would he let go of it, for "as my mind caught hold upon this thought," he says, "I cried within my heart: O Jesus, thou Son of God, have mercy on me, who am in the gall of bitterness, and am encircled about by the everlasting chains of death" (Alma 36:18). That's how Alma was convinced of his sins, how he found mercy, and how he obtained forgiveness — as Paul did, as Enos did, as Joseph Smith did, as every genuine convert does. Thus Alma, like all authentic converts, exemplifies many recurring themes of conversion: he obtained a revealed conviction of his own sins, acquired redeeming faith in Christ as his only Savior, repented of all personal sinfulness, came to the Father in the name of his Son seeking the help no one else could provide, besought the Father through repentance and faith in his Son for mercy and forgiveness, obtained mercy and a revealed witness from the Father that his sins were forgiven, and found "the peace of God, which passeth all understanding" and brought rest to his troubled soul (Philip. 4:7). For "when I thought this," Alma continues, "I could remember my pains no more; yea, I was harrowed up by the memory of my sins no more" (Alma 36:19). That's an exceptional and important thing: a moment ago he remembered all of his sins, but now he remembers none of them; so, what goes on here? Well, God was merciful to Alma and forgave his sins, that's what. "And oh," he tells us, "what joy and what marvelous light I did behold; yea, my soul was filled with joy as exceeding as was my pain" (Alma 36:20). He had never experienced anything more bitter than his pain and knew of nothing sweeter than his joy; and when he envisioned God sitting on his throne amidst throngs of praising angels, Alma — the same man who wanted to be banished and become extinct in order to avoid the presence of God — now says, "My soul did long to be there" (Alma 36:22). Like Enos before him and Joseph after him, he declares solemnly: "I know that . . . [God] will raise me up at the last day," and "I will praise him forever" (Alma 36:28).

## V. Brief Conclusion

Since no one, as authentic converts inevitably insist, can know any of this *except* by revelation, the revealed witness of personal sinfulness is essential to all conversions, as is the revealed witness of forgiveness to everyone who is converted. Because being properly convinced of our sins is so important, accordingly, this paper not only began but has continued and now ends with a crucial declaration by the Lord himself to his first modern apostles; for it is "by your hands," he tells them plainly, that "I will work a marvelous work among the children of men, unto the convincing of many of their sins, that they may come unto repentance, and that they may come unto the kingdom of my Father" (D&C 18:44). Convincing us of our sins is therefore the proper work of Christ, who wants to redeem us from sin on conditions of repentance and faith in him; and his work must never be confused with the unholy work of nefarious spirits who attempt the same thing in order to destroy hope in us, or with the profitable work of modern snake oil salesmen who do it because it makes self-help remedies sell like hotcakes and turns their get-rich-quick schemes into stock market successes. It is thus the Lord's own great and marvelous work, and his *alone*, that brings us to redeeming faith, sincere repentance, and actual forgiveness by convincing us of our sins; and except the Lord do the convincing, there is no redemption: there is only condemnation, for

Deny it as thou wilt,
They also work in vain
That labor mightily for gain
To ease the unrelenting pain
Of unforgiven guilt.[35]

# Notes

1. Paul's preconversion sinfulness is amply documented in Acts 9:1-2; 22:4-5; 26:9-12; and elsewhere.

2. Paul's sinfulness: Acts 9:1-2; 22:4-5; 26:9-12; the sudden flashing light: 9:3; 22:6; 26:13; blinded by the light: 9:8-9; 22:11; falls to the ground: 9:4; 22:7; hears a voice speaking in Hebrew: 9:4; 22:7; 26:14; conversation with the Lord: 9:4-6; 22:7-8, 10; 26:15-18; rises to his feet: 9:8-9; 22:11, 16; 26:16; the sequel in Damascus: 9:10-19; 22:12-16. Information about Paul's companions on the road to Damascus is slightly contradictory as follows: they saw the light: 22:9; stood speechless (in 9:7) but fell to the ground (in 26:14); heard the voice (in 9:7) but did not hear the voice (in 22:9); and saw no one: 9:7. That Christ appeared to Paul, who actually *saw* him, is confirmed in 1 Cor. 15:8 and elsewhere.

3. Translating ἰδεῖν τὸν Δίκαιον as "to see his Just One," since the definite article often functions as a possessive pronoun but cannot function as a demonstrative pronoun and does not mean "that" (as in the KJV).

4. The basic meaning of ἄξιος is "weighty," or better, "weighing the same as"; it implies that something is freighted with significance because it's "worthy of grave consideration," it "carries its own weight," it's "worth its weight in gold," etc.

5. "Worthy of all acceptation" is a mechanical translation of the Vulgate's *omni acceptione dignus:* it does not do justice to πάσης ἀποδοχῆς ἄξιος, which means "worthy of total acceptance" or "requiring absolute acceptance."

6. Alma the Elder, who spent his early days and nights doing who knows what as a priest of King Noah, was also convinced of his sins by the preaching of Abinadi. "Remember the iniquity of king Noah and his priests," he says, adding that "I myself [as one of his priests] was caught in a snare, and did many things which were abominable in the sight of the Lord, which caused me sore repentance; nevertheless, after much tribulation, the Lord did hear my cries, and did answer my prayers. . . . [But] in this I do not glory, for I am unworthy to glory of myself" (Mosiah 23:9-11).

7. This is a partial line from Edward H. Bickersteth, *Yesterday, To-day, and For Ever; a Poem in Twelve Books* (London: Rivingtons, 1878), 229–30. The segment of this lengthy poem excerpted here reads as follows:

> As the load immense, intolerable,
> Of the world's sin,
> Casting its dreadful shadow high as heaven,
> Deep as Gehenna, nearer and more near
> Grounded at last upon that sinless soul
> With all its crushing weight and killing curse,
> Then first, from all eternity then first,
> From his Beloved Son the Father's face
> Was slowly averted,
> And its light eclipsed.

8. Translating πρὸς ὑποτύπωσιν τῶν μελλόντων ἐπ᾽ αὐτῷ εἰς ζωὴν αἰώνιον from 1 Tim. 1:16. This formative pattern requires explanation: it is translated from πρὸς ὑποτύπωσιν in Greek, which means "in view of hypotyposis," and from *ad informationem* in Latin, which means "unto informing" or "with a view toward the formation of something in," and both phrases obscure what Paul means by saying that his conversion establishes a pattern out of which, or following which, all authentic conversions occur. "Hypotyposis" and "hypotypical" appear in English as naturalized concepts whose initial element, ὑπό, has the meaning of *sub*, its Latin equivalent, which means "under" or "underneath" as in "*sub*marine." But that makes ὑπό behave like *sub* in "*sub*standard," as though something that isn't up to snuff were unacceptable. "Hypotyposis" has therefore become a technical term for the flowery description of anything which, though vividly picturesque, is inadequate because its adequacy is obscured by rhetoric; and "hypotypical" means "subtypical" in the sense of being only partly typical, insufficiently typical, or somehow less than fully typical. But we must not be misled by modern meanings imported into traditional concepts. This idea of "under," meaning *sub* as in "*sub*standard," has nothing to do with Paul's use of ὑποτύπωσιν, since we cannot interpret ancient words by their modern connotations.

9. A perfect example of what happens when Greek words are naturalized in English is our word "cosmetic." It derives from κοσμητικός, which means "pertaining to order," and because the cosmos was an orderly thing and order was loved by the Greeks, it has notions of beauty in it. But κοσμητικός comes into English as "cosmetic" through its 25th or 30th connotation, since κοσμέω, among a whole flock of other things, can mean "imposing order on the face," and once it comes into English that way, "cosmetic" refers to "cosmetics" and cannot be used to mean "cosmic" in phrases like "cosmetic theories" or "cosmetic wonder."

10. That may be startling, but it's what ὑποτύπωσις means, and if we consult the Latin text of this passage, it's also startling to find that Paul's conversion was accomplished *ad informationem* — until we realize that he was speaking the formal language of Greek philosophy, and that the basic element of *in-FORMA-tio,* from which we get "in-FORMA-tion," is *forma.* And since *forma* is an important Latin word that translates all the "forms" of Greek philosophy, the *formae* constitute the intellectual patterns, as opposed to the empirical contents, of Greek thought that philosophers have never ceased talking about. The Latin word *forma,* incidentally, translates two Greek words that mean "spirit," but "spirit" doesn't mean the same thing in Greek thought that it means in Christianity. It means "nonphysical" in classical philosophy because it describes something that has no chemistry, something that does not exist in a physical way but creates "spiritual" patterns that only the mind can "see" in the world and utilize within itself. These *formae* are the philosophical patterns known as "forms," and that is what confronts us here. *Forma,* accordingly, stands for two Greek words, εἶδος and ἰδέα. If we transliterate ἰδέα we get "idea"; and here again we must be careful, since we think of ideas as subsistents in our minds whereas Plato's ἰδέαι are existents in the world. Both of these words, however, are derived from the root ἰδ- "see," but there are two ways to see: the philosophical way of seeing refers to the mind's "spiritual" vision, to its way of seeing the essential significance of things, not merely to its empirical capacity for detecting fluctuations of matter and energy by means of its bodily senses. This is the seeing of intelligence, the way a human mind sees things "spiritually" through its own insights, not by revelation or by means of its sensory organs. *Forma,* in a word, is rational insight. It describes *the rational spirit of definity* that makes anything thought or sensed by human beings intelligible; without that spirit of definity, which establishes the limits of human rationality, nothing anyone could think about or detect in the world by means of the senses would be intellectible. The Greek spirit of rational definity, it goes without saying, must not be confused with Roman notions of infinity, which the Greeks do not discuss: their concern with definity and indefinity is definitely *not* the Roman concern with finitude and infinity. Anyone perusing the parallel lists of the Pythagoreans, who enumerate what's "good" and "bad" in Greek thought, sees immediately that definity is equated with "good" and indefinity with "evil," since the good list contains only defined or definite things, while everything amorphous, indefinite, or undefined is in the bad list. These Greco-Latin words for "spirit" constitute whatever it is that "forms" or constrains a thing to be what it is and prevents it from being anything else. The "form" of a fern is thus its essential nature, the thing that makes a fern a fern and not a rose, or a hedgehog, or an orchid, or a lizard, or a tomato; and everything comes down to its patterned definity, to the nature of its definers and definitions.

11. Ammon, who went through this conversion process himself, recognized at least eight things in it when "king Lamoni was under the power of God; he knew *that* the dark veil of unbelief was being cast away from his mind,"

*that* "the light which did light up his mind . . . was the light of the glory of God," *that* it was "a marvelous light of his goodness," *that* it "had infused . . . joy into his soul," *that* "the cloud of darkness . . . [had] been dispelled," *that* "the light of everlasting life was lit up in his soul," *that* "this had overcome his natural frame," and *that* "he was carried away in God" (Alma 19:6; emphasis added).

12. That is also what *ad informationem* means if we discount the modern connotations of empirical content in our word "information." When Jerome used that phrase in the fourth century A.D. to translate πρὸς ὑποτύπωσιν, he did so because its verb, *informo*, like the Greek verb ὑποτυπόω, means "to create form in," with everything that implies. Thus *informatio*, too, refers to something, whatever it is, in which, or within which, the nature of anything is formed, shaped, structured, established, identified, and authenticated. These Greco-Latin phrases refer, each in its own way, to the formative matrix that creates the inner structural nature of anything that comes out of it. Since I've been involved professionally with "information science," I might add, I'm very much aware that electrical engineers, who study the movement of electromagnetic particles along wires or ionized pathways in the atmosphere, think they are studying "information" — which means that scientific thinking about information as electromagnetic particles, as empirical data to be studied in laboratories, has replaced the old definition of information-as-ideas with its new definition of information-as-particles. Thus, information is no longer something in the mind: it is something in the world, something in the physical mechanics of atoms in motion that can be observed, measured, manipulated, and analyzed. We live today with this new scientific understanding of mathematizable information as data, which makes it virtually impossible to understand traditional concepts of *informatio* as something consisting of forms or ideas.

13. By changing the *scale* of the pattern, which does not alter the pattern itself, any seamstress can make dresses of different sizes to fit dolls, little girls, big girls, young ladies, middle-aged matrons, and older women; and the pattern remains unchanged if some dresses are made of silk, some of rayon, others of cotton, and still others of numerous other materials. So, too, every performance of the same play is different from any other, since it varies perforce in such matters as the time, place, audience, scenery, actors, and staging directions of its production. And "God Bless America" is perceived as the same tune whether sung by a man or a woman, played on a violin or a flute, or performed by a string quartet or a symphony orchestra — even though acoustical scientists can easily show that no two notes of like physical frequency are shared by any of its renditions.

14. Cf. George Q. Cannon, *Gospel Truth: Discourses and Writings of President George Q. Cannon*, ed. Jerreld L. Newquist (Salt Lake City: Deseret Book, 1987), 1:127: "Gospel principles [are the] same in all ages. If it was necessary in the days of Jesus and of His Apostles that men should believe in Jesus and

repent of their sins, it is necessary today; and no human judgment nor human council can do away with that necessity. . . . As God did make faith in Jesus . . . necessary for man's salvation, it is still necessary. . . . This has not changed. It cannot be changed. . . . There may be any amount of enlightenment, of wisdom, and of knowledge, but however great this may be, it does not affect in the slightest degree the principle that men must believe in Jesus as the foundation of their faith and of their salvation. They must also repent of their sins. No sophistry, no human wisdom, no human device can remove . . . the necessity of the repentance of sin; the Gospel of Jesus Christ demands absolutely that sin . . . must be repented of." Cf. Brigham Young: "There never was a prophet on the earth but what was subject to passions, as we are. Every son and daughter of Adam that has come into this world has been subject to sin, and prone to wander," *Journal of Discourses,* 8:352.

15. This statement appears three times verbatim in Alma 11:41; 12:18; and Moro. 7:38. See also Mosiah 16:5.

16. See Dean C. Jessee, "The Early Accounts of Joseph Smith's First Vision," *BYU Studies* 9, no. 3 (spring, 1969), 275–94; and consult Milton V. Backman, *Joseph Smith's First Vision; the First Vision in its Historical Context* (Salt Lake City: Bookcraft, 1971). This is not the later account, familiar from its publication in the Pearl of Great Price, which came out of the Nauvoo period.

17. From an edited text issued by The Church of Jesus Christ of Latter-day Saints in its *Presidents of the Church* (student manual for Rel. 345 prepared by Institutes of the Church, Salt Lake City, 1979), 30–31. Joseph Smith's six-page history uses the word "convicted" rather than "convinced" in this statement. Since both words derive from Latin *convincio, convincere, convici,convictus* and mean essentially the same thing. Its editors, however, who often follow modern preferences, have probably chosen the best alternative.

18. To those Latter-day Saints who confuse their ameliorated humanism with "spirituality," Joseph Smith should be like Norman Vincent Peale, not like Paul, since, to reverse an old quip by Adlai Stevenson, they find Saint Peale appealing and Saint Paul appalling. As a colleague once told me, on hearing Ernest L. Wilkinson laud the learned Dr. Peale to the skies at BYU, "they confuse Mormonism with Normanism."

19. This sequence is clearly discernible in Enos and elsewhere in the Book of Mormon. See, for example, 3 Ne. 28:8–9, 38; 4 Ne. 1:44; Morm. 2:12–15, 19, 27; and Morm. 5:8–11.

20. As in D&C 18:44, which we frequently refer to in this paper.

21. "There shall be no other name given nor any other way nor means whereby salvation can come unto the children of men, only in and through the name of Christ, the Lord Omnipotent," Mosiah 3:17.

22. Enos wasn't merely a deer hunter in our sense. He was hunting beasts "in the forests"; and since "forests" is plural, this was no sporting romp on opening day in a specific forest: days go by in this narrative, as Enos goes from forest to forest on an extended hunt for food, which his people sorely needed in order to survive.

23. Enos says in verse 2 that his wrestling occurred "before I received a *remission* of my sins," whereas the Lord tells him in verse 5 "thy sins are *forgiven* thee" — which clearly shows that "remission" and "forgiveness" are the same thing: to have our sins remitted is to have our sins forgiven.

24. In 1949–51, Elder Spencer W. Kimball, who frequently visited the Southwest Indian Mission, told us time and again something like this: "Now look, elders, you're not down here just playing around. The Lamanites must have the gospel. It *has* to come to them." He spoke frequently about Enos and others in the Book of Mormon, whose earnest prayers were that the Nephite scriptures might be preserved to come unto the Lamanites. I still have, among my souvenirs from those days, a long list of excerpts from Book of Mormon prophets to this effect that I compiled at BYU and sent to Elder Kimball in the early fifties, together with a gracious letter from him in which he acknowledged once again the importance of such utterances by Enos and other prophets and the great responsibility of the Latter-day Saints in helping to bring about their fulfillment.

25. This statement is not solely about the nature of the Lamanites. All who allow themselves to be led by their evil nature will become wild, ferocious, bloodthirsty, etc., since the fallen nature of man is like that — it will lead anyone who follows it away from God.

26. This and similar passages in the Book of Mormon meant a lot to Elder Kimball, who emphasized them time and again to the Lamanite missionaries of the Southwest Indian Mission.

27. Tracing "the sceptical tradition . . . from the seventeenth century [A.D.] to the present" includes an account of "the French Revolution, which witnessed the first concerted effort in the modern West to dechristianize a whole society and to institutionalize scepticism," Franklin L. Baumer, *Religion and the Rise of Scepticism* (New York: Harcourt, Brace, 1960), 22. This effort is described at length in "Crush the Infamous Thing," the first chapter of ibid., 35–77.

28. The way this is stated suggests that these young rebels regarded God as a pious fiction to be ruthlessly exposed and the king as personifying the only "real" power they acknowledged — the formidable power of the Nephite state.

29. To Helaman in Alma 36:1–30; to Shiblon in Alma 38:5–9; and doubtless elsewhere to Corianton, possibly in such passages as Alma 29:1–17, etc. There

is an important third-person account of Alma's conversion in Mosiah 27:1–37, which may also be consulted; but the other references listed here are all to first-person accounts.

30. Adding that "I did cry unto him and I did find peace to my soul." There are many things that only those who are born of God can know; and one of them is that their sins are forgiven.

31. "Do not say," he advised Shiblon and others, "that we are better than our brethren; but rather say: O Lord, forgive my unworthiness, and remember my brethren in mercy — yea, acknowledge your unworthiness before God at all times" (Alma 38:14).

32. We think it should say: "If thou wilt *not* of thyself be destroyed, seek no more to destroy the church of God"; for otherwise it means: "If you want to be destroyed, don't try to destroy the church" — which makes no sense at all.

33. Cf. Nephi's "O wretched man that I am!" in 2 Ne. 4:17.

34. This meaning derives from the suppressed apodosis of certain conditional sentences in Hebrew and its cognate languages. The apodosis (then-clause) is omitted in these sentences because the protasis (if-clause) is sufficient in itself to imply something like "or else!" or "beware!" or "watch out!" — which functions as an unexpressed then-clause suggesting that something ominous will happen whenever conditions in the if-clause are met. Thus, the exasperated mother (who comes into the kitchen and finds her precocious four-year-old boy teetering on a chair perched on a table trying to get a cookie from a jar she hid from him on the highest shelf she could reach) may exclaim: "Oh, Billy! If you don't get out of that cookie jar!" — and that's all she has to say. Or, we might tell our own children: "If you don't do your homework, . . ." And so on. The point is that this is the normal way to state conditional sentences like these in many Near Eastern languages.

35. I have penned these lines to express the spirit of Psalms 127:1, "Except the Lord build the house, they labour in vain that build it," and of 2 Ne. 26:31, "The laborer in Zion shall labor for Zion; for if they labor for money they shall perish."